RESCUED
READINGS

RESCUED READINGS

A Reconstruction

of

GERTRUDE STEIN'S

Difficult Texts

Elizabeth Fifer

 Wayne State University Press   Detroit

Library of Congress Cataloging-in-Publication Data

Fifer, Elizabeth.
    Rescued readings : a reconstruction of Gertrude Stein's
difficult texts / Elizabeth Fifer.
        p.   cm.
    Includes bibliographical references and index.
    ISBN 0-8143-2340-5 (alk. paper)
    1. Stein, Gertrude, 1874–1946—Criticism and
interpretation.   I. Title.
PS3537.T323Z589   1992
818'.5209—dc20   92-7291
                                                      CIP

Book design by Joanne E. Kinney

Kindness necessarily swims in a bottom with a razor which needs powder powder that makes a top be in the middle and necessarily not indicate a kind of collection, a collection of more or more gilt and mostly blue pipes pipes which are bound bound with old oil and mustard exact mustard which means that yellow is obtained. Gracious oh my cold under fur, under no rescued reading.

—"A Sweet Tail," *Geography and Plays*

Contents

█

Acknowledgments

I thank the editors of the following journals for their encouragement and support. Versions of some chapters, some considerably altered, have appeared in various journals: parts of Chapter 1 in the *University of Michigan Papers in Women's Studies*; Chapter 2 in *SIGNS: A Journal of Women in Culture and Society* Vol. 4, No. 3, copyright 1979 by the University of Chicago Press; Chapter 3 in *Texas Studies in Literature and Languages* Vol. 24, No. 4, Winter 1982, the University of Texas Press; Chapter 4 in *The Journal of Narrative Technique* Vol. 10, No. 2, Spring 1980, Eastern Michigan University; Chapter 6 in *Modern Fiction Studies* Vol. 34, No. 3, copyright 1988 by Purdue Research Foundation, West Lafayette, Indiana, 47907, Reprinted with permission.

I am grateful to the Collection of American Literature, Beinecke Rare Book and Manuscript Library, Yale University, for allowing me to study and quote from "The Notebooks for *The Making of Americans*" in the Gertrude Stein Collection. This book was made possible by released time and research grants from Lehigh University.

I offer thanks to Lucy Bednar, my research assistant, and to Christine Roysden, Head of Information Services, Lehigh University Libraries. Annette Benert, James Frakes, Edward Gallagher, Michael J. Hoffman, and Daniel Ross offered expert assistance as I approached the final draft. I owe much to Richard Bridgman and Catharine Stimpson for their illuminating scholarship and kind support. Special thanks to Kenneth Fifer for his help at every stage of this project.

9

Abbreviations

▬

Quotations from Gertrude Stein's works are cited in the text using the following abbreviations and short titles; when lines are sufficiently located by the title of a short work or a short section of a work, no additional citation appears:

AB   *Alphabets and Birthdays.* Yale Series of the Unpublished Writings of Gertrude Stein 7. Ed. Carl Van Vechten. New Haven: Yale University Press, 1957.

AFAM   *As Fine As Melanctha.* Yale Series of the Unpublished Writings of Gertrude Stein 4. Ed. Carl Van Vechten. New Haven: Yale University Press, 1954.

BTV   *Bee Time Vine and Other Pieces.* Yale Series of the Unpublished Writings of Gertrude Stein 3. Ed. Carl Van Vechten. New Haven: Yale University Press, 1953.

EA   *Everybody's Autobiography.* New York: Random House, 1937.

GP   *Geography and Plays.* 1922. New York: Something Else Press, 1968.

LO&P   *Last Operas and Plays.* Ed. Carl Van Vechten. New York: Rinehart, 1949.

11

OP   *Operas and Plays.* Paris: Plain Editions, 1932.

PL   *Painted Lace and Other Pieces.* Yale Series of the Unpublished
         Writings of Gertrude Stein 5. Ed. Carl Van Vechten. New
         Haven: Yale University Press, 1955.

TWO   *Two and Other Early Portraits.* Yale Series of the Unpublished
         Writings of Gertrude Stein 1. Ed. Carl Van Vechten. New
         Haven: Yale University Press, 1951.

UK   *Useful Knowledge.* 1929. New York: American Alpine Club,
         1972.

Introduction
Reading Gertrude Stein

Gertrude Stein's texts provoke readers. This book, which concentrates on the interaction of her lesbianism and her art, emphasizes the dynamics of this provocation. The relationship between sexuality and textuality deserves our attention, not least because Stein's use of her homosexuality as a subject for her work has too long isolated her, making her texts "unreadable."

We live in a century in which readers who felt able to accept, at least for literary purposes, Jarry's violence, Artaud's cruelty, Beckett's exhaustion, and Celine's fascism, seemed to draw the line at Stein's lesbian displays. Better that it should mean nothing than that it should mean *that* seems too often to have been the response. Critics preferred to focus on her "nonsensical" grammatical usages rather than to encounter directly her sexually charged content. Today, Stein still remains marginal, an anomaly, even in liberated zones of the intellect and spirit, like the Left Bank, the expatriate community where she lived and wrote from 1903 to 1947. It was left to Yale University Press to publish many of her important writings after her death, in the outstanding *Yale Series of The Unpublished Works of Gertrude Stein* (1951–58).

The recovery of these texts—I mean, of our ability to read them—begins with Richard Bridgman's *Gertrude Stein in Pieces* in 1970, a literary biography that created a whole generation of American Stein scholars. I find Bridgman's text to be a revelation, full of possibilities for further study, and I am fascinated at how his work charts Stein's fears, anxieties, and vulnerabilities throughout each stage of her life and work. I admire the way Bridgman combines apt literary quotation with a substantial discussion of biography to confront directly the questions of identity at the source of Stein's fears (94) and his direct exploration of Stein's attitude toward her homosexuality.

Bridgman recognizes how Stein uses encoded sexual reference throughout her difficult texts (148). Early in his book, he notes that "it is in the process of taming and exorcising her demons that Gertrude Stein's stylistic course was irrevocably set" (27). He demonstrates how "verbal substitution eventually became an important feature of Gertrude Stein's style" (56), and he links this "evasiveness" (56) to Stein's fear of discovery of forbidden sexual desires and acts, noting that "lesbian sentiments contributed to Gertrude Stein's impenetrability" (106).

Edmund Wilson was the first to observe something of this kind in *Shores of Light* (1952), in which he attributes Stein's stylistic peculiarities to "a need imposed by the problem of writing about relationships between women of a kind that standards of that era would not have allowed her to describe more explicitly" (581). Bridgman develops and expands this idea by demonstrating how Stein's obscurity protected her "concealed confessions" (227) not only from a homophobic culture but from Stein's own internal censor and from Alice B. Toklas herself (145). Knowing that Stein confessed to using private language (106), Bridgman glosses many of her "false names," her " 'way of naming things . . . without naming them' " (255).

Linda Simon's *Biography of Alice B. Toklas* (1977), and its perceptive appendix, "An Annotated Gertrude Stein," also deserves special mention. Complementing Bridgman, Simon's literary biography uses Stein's literary works to illuminate Toklas's life and her relationship with Stein. Simon introduces many themes and ideas, mostly about the nature of Stein's sexuality, that I have tried to incorporate into my work.

More recently, in *Women of the Left Bank* (1986), cultural historian Shari Benstock has further clarified Stein's work and life by contextualizing her within her Left Bank milieu. Many of Benstock's observations on period homophobia and misogyny help explain Stein's own repulsion toward women and homosexuality: "Most of the women of the Left Bank community . . . demonstrated that they had internalized both homophobia and misogyny" (115). Female homosexuals often had a "destructive and homophobic literary and social self-image"

(11). By detailing Stein's life and her world, and her salon and friend-ship circle, and by analyzing her attitudes toward herself and others, Benstock has given us a fresh critical perspective on the texts.

My work has been directly influenced by Catharine Stimpson, whose series of essays on Stein's identity seem to me exemplary femi-nist scholarship. I find particularly convincing her vision of Stein's self-hatred, through a recognition of her "anomalous" nature and body and the "impurity" of her sexual identification ("The Mind, the Body, and Gertrude Stein," 1977) and the "monstrosity" of her desires ("The Somagrams of Gertrude Stein," 1985). Stimpson identifies the de-stabilizing and subversive elements of Stein's life with the language she used ("Gertrude Stein and the Transposition of Gender," 1986). She best captures Stein's divided nature in the complexities of her life with Alice B. Toklas, in which they obeyed heterosexual norms in a homo-sexual marriage ("Gertrice/Altrude: Stein, Toklas, and the Paradox of the Happy Marriage," 1984).

Stimpson addresses important questions of meaning in Stein. In "Gertrude Stein and the Transposition of Gender," she speaks of Stein's "laboratory of the text" (4) in which Stein "rearranges" gender's "orders, codes, and poses" (2) from the standpoint of a lesbian writer. While Stein's inability to fit into any one culturally defined role gave her writing more freedom and flexibility, and while Stein was deeply conscious of language's self-referential qualities, "she also believed in the writer as representor, in language as representational and referen-tial" (7).

I am encouraged that Stimpson sees in Stein's texts a language of desire that grounds its polyvalent, multidimensional nature in ques-tions of sexual identity. Characterizing the kind of text that Stein, along with other modern women of her day, were creating, she writes that "the texts such women generated were often coded rather than open, sublimated rather than straightforward, hazy with metaphors and silence rather than lucid" (1977, 505).

In addition to these critics who have shaped my own views on Stein, I would also mention other significant contributions to the ongoing discussion of Stein's difficult texts. Cynthia Secor, in "Ida, A Great American Novel" (1978), discusses Stein's *Ida*, a text in which the protagonist's search for a separate female identity is of paramount concern. In "Gertrude Stein: The Complex Force of Her Femininity" (1982), Secor tries to distinguish Stein from the male modernists like Ezra Pound, T.S. Eliot, and James Joyce, on the basis of her rejection of patriarchal myth (31). Secor sees Stein's style as taking her beyond gender, attributing Stein's success in avoiding myth to her challenging stylistic decisions: "By refusing to engage in plots, by treating types rather than genders, by writing metaphysical rather than dramatic poetry, and by doing portraits and theater rather than narrative, Stein escaped stylistically the net of gender" (32).

In "The Question of Gertrude Stein" (1982), Secor again argues that Stein's work moves "beyond gender and ethnic categories" (304) and quotes Stein from *The Geographical History of America* (1936): "I had to capture the value of the individual word, find out what it meant and act within it" (100). This essay is particularly effective in its effort to chart "how the human mind composes, derives significance from the irrational, the ordinary" (308). Secor's vision of Stein is a kind of corrective for the more negative attributes noted by other critics, including myself. She reminds the reader that Stein's fundamental values—"feminine, sensual, domestic, nurturing, healing" (308)—can too easily be overlooked.

Lisa Ruddick, discussing erotic encoding in "A Rosy Charm: Gertrude Stein and the Repressed Feminine" (1986), finds that Stein's codes concern "gender and culture" (225) as well as sexuality. She uses psychoanalytic tools to gloss imagery of menstruation and defloration in *Tender Buttons* (226), a text that she finds "recovering the mother" (237). She analyzes Stein's shifting attitudes and notes how Stein reverses values and disrupts hierarchies in an effort to include "unconscious" forces in her writing.

Marianne DeKoven's *A Different Language: Gertrude Stein's Experimental Writing* (1983) argues that "with experimental writing . . . we cannot generate thematic syntheses at all" (6). Like Ruddick, she uses the figure of the mother as a location for Stein's language, employing Kristeva and Derrida to contrast conventional patriarchal speech with pre-symbolic, pre-oedipal, and maternal experimental speech. While DeKoven rightly stresses the importance of Stein's experimental writing, I differ with her assertion that "it is clear that Stein considers communicated content irrelevant to value in art" (24). At other times, her arguments parallel my own, as in her observation that "obliteration and intensification of meaning oscillate for the reader" (111). While uneasy with the idea of Stein's "literary rebellion . . . in language itself *rather than* in thematic content" (111; my italics), I certainly agree with her conclusion that, for Stein, "if patriarchy is to be transformed at all, it must be transformed not only at its most visible levels (political, social, economic, cultural) *but also* at the fundamental or radical level of the structures of language which enable meaning" (149–50; my italics).

Because I believe the Steinian text is accessible to readers, I differ with Benstock's conclusion that Stein's meaning is not determinant (1986, 161), that Stein breaks the pact, using Neil Schmitz's terms (1983), between text and reader, that she relinquishes the right to make language submit to her will (Benstock 1986, 159). All these things have been said about a great variety of writers, and I am not sure how or whether they apply distinctively to Stein. Neither does it differentiate her work from that of other modernists with whom she might be grouped, especially writers like Alfred Jarry, Samuel Beckett, Louis-Ferdinand Celine, Flann O'Brien, and even Eugene Ionesco, all of whom, like Stein, purposefully and openly disrupt the relation between reader and text. While what Benstock says about Stein's play with signifiers and her quarrel with convention is thoughtful, the idea of writing without will is difficult to comprehend. Is it possible to relinquish conscious control over writing? Every writer would like greater access to the tumult of creativity assumed to inhabit the unconscious mind, but to consciously will that access may not be achievable. Stein, like other writers, seizes on any and every possible source of inspiration available; she does so because, like other writers, she keenly needs to communicate.

Harriet Chessman's recent work, *The Public is Invited to Dance: Representation, the Body, and Dialogue in Gertrude Stein* (1989), employs the pre-symbolic, pre-oedipal, anti-gender, and anti-hierarchical terms of Ruddick and DeKoven. Like Ruddick, she argues that Stein's texts are meaningful: "Her language is never simply non-signifying or disruptive of signification. . . . Stein's writing mixes the figurative and the literal, the symbolic and the bodily" (4). Following my example in "Guardians and Witnesses" (1980), Chessman charts an intimate, not exclusively lover-to-lover dialogue of "plural voices" that has the erotic as one of its elements (4). Like Marjorie Perloff ("Poetry as Word-System," 1979), she believes that Stein meaningfully took "words out of their usual contexts and created new relationships among them" (75).

Stein critics will continue to chart a difficult path between an overdetermined and a random text, between what is meaningful and what is not, between what is acceptable and what is not. It is my hope that this book will add something of value to that discussion. What I see in Gertrude Stein's difficult texts is that, regardless of the particularities of the time or place of their production, her erotic subject produces similar patterns of complex language and experimental narrative strategies. This book argues that we can learn to "read" these patterns and strategies, just as we can "decode" Stein's conscious manipulation of an oblique vocabulary of lesbian eroticism, in order to deepen our appreciation of Stein's art.

The particular literary works under discussion are those generally known as "difficult," and include parts of the *Yale Edition of The Unpublished Writings* (from *Two, Bee Time Vine, As Fine As Melanctha, Painted Lace, Stanzas In Meditation*, and *Alphabets and Birthdays*); three volumes of her plays, *Geography and Plays, Operas and Plays, Last Operas and Plays;* and one prose work, *Useful Knowledge*. This body of work, as I have observed, has traditionally troubled and puzzled Stein's readers. Rather than turning away from meaning, I see the difficult writings as those in which Stein most fully expresses her deepest feelings. Though the reader must at times feel overwhelmed by the sheer force and variety of experimentation, Stein uses her techniques in order to communicate, be it in a particular and complex way.

Stein's manipulation of narrative technique and nontraditional language remains susceptible to the widest variety of possible readings. To rob her texts of this sort of dimensionality would be to undermine their literary status. But it is also true that, taken together, Stein's repeated stylistic patterns are linked to her need to at once reveal and conceal her erotic and homosexual content. In the difficult texts, one important way of reading Stein is as a specifically homosexual writer for whom questions of gender necessitate and shape literary experimentation.

That these texts consistently challenge expected representational strategies does not turn them into nonsemantic abstractions. Without denying their many other important qualities—I do not agree with Ulla E. Dydo when she asserts, "if [Stein's] language is read as a lesbian code, her work becomes restricted to a single dimension" (1985, 279)—we must not mistake the fact that these texts are obsessively sexual, rooted in the author's biography, and that they reflect a complex but definite emotional and artistic agenda. This book will show how certain recurrent images, for instance, those drawn from her domestic and social environment, reappear throughout, unifying and directing the reader's response.

Most of the experience of literature confirms the proposition that ambivalence heightens and enhances meaning rather than cancels it. In her difficult texts, an intimate odyssey that represents the life work of a major American writer, Stein addresses significant human questions of sexuality and identity.

Stein should not be read like Eliot or Pound or Joyce. Indeed, the difficulties of her work involve her general rejection of the modernist conventions that have shaped our customary reading methods. Stein rejects the notion of economy of language at the heart of literary modernism. In its place, she substitutes a love of *copia*, the belief that no catalogue can be too long or various for the human condition. Like Baroque art, Stein's difficult texts elevate process over product, validating a seemingly unbalanced construct of countervailing and opposing tensions, usually close to those of spoken language, caught in the processes of formulating meaning. Though initially overwhelmed by the rejection of classical harmonies—shocked, if need be, to attention— the reader's perception of local disorder and contradiction is finally subsumed by an appreciation of a larger and more complex unity.

A discussion of Stein's non-modernist principles, employing the model of Derrida and the deconstructionists, is Shari Benstock's "Beyond the Reaches of Feminist Criticism" ([1984] 1987). As Benstock notes, "her writing followed language to its farthest point, a zero-degree where language and external reality split forever from each other, a moment at which language constituted itself beyond observable reality" (25). This, however, may only describe the first half of a longer voyage—after reaching such a zero point, both reader and writer must journey back home again. As Benstock also remarks: "Stein's perverse style has intimate connections to her lesbianism, which is the motivating force for this private language, at odds with any accepted forms of meaning, a language exploring *seemingly* arbitrary and coincidental links between signifier and signified" (19; my italics).

Like Lawrence or Joyce, Stein chose to work in an essentially autobiographical context characterized by a more frank treatment of sexuality than had been available in the years before World War I. To the celebration of sensuality, however, is appended an element of defensiveness, of fear and repulsion. While exploring the licentious new world of the modernists, her most important work has more to do with her own ambivalences within a hostile environment. This book argues that the significance of Stein's manipulation of language lies in her use of its disguising properties.

Stein's desire to hide her meaning or to multiply it can be as simple as her use of double meanings or as complex as her densest associative catalogues. Even as she invites us to dismiss her erotic content as pure banality or to experience it as joyous word-play, she means it to be the reader's duty, nearly always, to go beyond this first response. It is this quality that transforms the usual relationship between reader and text and gives these works their particular effect, setting them apart from the more conventional literary efforts that made her public reputation, such as *The Autobiography Of Alice B. Toklas, Wars I Have Seen*, and *Everybody's Autobiography*.

Rescued Readings, like Caesar's Gaul, is divided into three parts, each one an attempt, as Stein would say, to "seize her." Chapter 1 presents an introduction to Stein's manifest and hidden texts as it attempts an overview of intention and technique, exploring the defensive mechanisms of key texts from different points in Stein's career. By understanding the intensity of their disguised autobiographical context, readers can better appreciate how Stein's critique of women's roles and behavior is consistently related to both her self-analysis and search for identity and the particular nature of her stylistic and narrative strategies. In these ways, chapter 1 seeks to provide a rationale for verbal obfuscation within the framework of Stein's experience and self-perception.

Chapters 2, 3, and 4 explore the revealing and concealing modes of Stein's erotic language. Her disguises and evasions, though set in different contexts, represent a theater in which she is both participant and observer. Stein's repertoire of sexual expressions, her vocabulary of desire, and her stylistic techniques are seen as inventions to simultaneously distance and approach their "forbidden" subject matter. Guarded content and repression mark nearly every stage of Stein's career, dissociating language from its expected content. Examining plays written between 1915 and 1946, I use psychoanalytic language to trace their characteristic deformations and typical syntactical patterns.

Chapters 5 and 6 examine volumes from the Yale series (*Painted Lace And Other Pieces* [1914–1937], *Stanzas in Meditation* [1929–1933], *Alphabets And Birthdays* [1915–1940], and *Bee Time Vine* [1913–1927]) in terms of "gaps" or empty spaces between words, the breakdown in communication created by Stein's marginal status and ambivalent relationship to her audience, her "conversations" with readers and others, and the effect of her choosing the homosexual alliance as a specific paradigm for the relationship between reader and writer.

Readers will note that the methodology of this book places special emphasis on the elaboration of specific words, phrases, and images, often taken from flattened, repetitive, or seemingly banal larger units.

Employing psychoanalytic and reader-response techniques, it follows these "charged" words and images as they submerge and reappear a few sentences, paragraphs, pages, or even volumes later. (In all cases the ellipses within the passages quoted from Stein are my own.) The "interrupted" text that Stein offers her readers couples the forces of expression and repression. Nevertheless, uncensored material can explode into a "neutral" context without warning.

Many readers have noted how the eroticism of Stein's difficult texts critiques social interactions and conventions, creates an avant-garde and experimental style, raises questions of censorship and self-censorship, and celebrates and describes female domesticity and intimacy. This book argues that Stein's writings reveal a striking vulnerability; Stein's social situation, her personal marginality, shapes her writing style by controlling both her conception of her audience and her self-image. Radical reading strategies seem most appropriate to deal with the radical nature of her literary creations. The reconstruction of Gertrude Stein's difficult texts is the action of reader and writer making dangerous meaning together.

1

Father, Brother, Lover, Other
Gertrude Stein
and the Search for Identity

Father: Patriarchy and the Struggle for Change in
The Mother Of Us All

To begin near the end seems most appropriate to a consideration of Gertrude Stein's difficult texts, not only because this approximates Stein's own procedures, but also because *The Mother Of Us All*,[1] completed in 1946, a year before her death, although ostensibly about the achievements of Susan B. Anthony, feminist, social reformer, and champion of woman's suffrage, offers a revealing self-assessment of Stein's life and career. When Stein's identity as an artist is transposed onto the Susan B. Anthony role, aesthetic considerations can be overtly presented as social and political issues. Her self-proclaimed literary revolution is, in Stein's mind, indissoluably linked to Anthony's social revolution: "I do want what we have got, has it not gone, what made it live" (87).

As Anthony, Stein can again replay her family history, hostilely confronting both her father and her brother Leo. The "boresome" pontificating fathers of the play, especially Daniel Webster (a "bearded Daniel" who bears both her father's beard and his name), become vehicles for judging Stein's own father. Stein can likewise ridicule her interfering, negative brother Leo in her dramatic presentation of the play's brothers, especially Indiana Elliot's, who bears the Steinian nickname of "Herman" and who inevitably disapproves of his sister's

22

marriage. In much of Stein's writing, disguised autobiography is not so much a favored technique as it is a necessary condition for literary creation; "for Stein everything in her adult life became a subject for and was subjected to her art" (Benstock 1986, 14).

In the play's world, men have few virtues. They are "conservative, selfish . . . ugly . . . gullible" (60). Their agency is to fight, whether on the battlefield or on the podium, forever fearful of each other and of women's power (68; 80). Any association with them is liable to be tainted. Susan B. Anthony even questions heterosexual procreation, calling it a "puzzle":[2]

It is a puzzle, I am not puzzled but it is a puzzle,
if there are no children there are no men and women,
and if there are men and women, it is rather horrible,
and if it is rather horrible, then there are children. (85)

Susan B. Anthony is not puzzled for herself—she has made her choice not to marry in order to devote herself to the women's agenda. Her companion, Anne, who is no doubt enlisted both to represent and upbraid Stein's own Alice B. Toklas, values Anthony completely and unquestioningly, considering herself married "to what you have been to that one" (75).

As the play develops the theme of equality in marriage, Stein further intertwines the political with the social, literary, and personal. Susan B. Anthony wants to empower other women but fears they will become exactly like men when they get their rights (81). In the spirit of comedy, in which the couple is allowed to marry despite any initial familial objections, Indiana Elliot is joined to Jo the Loiterer ("let us dance and sing," 87). As they trade names to signal their utopian equality, Susan B. Anthony, symbol of the old guard, gives way to a new force, those reformers who will come after her, the inheritors of her political and social accomplishments.

As "the mother of us all," Stein must forge new possibilities for both masculine and feminine identities and defeat the powers of oppression. As an innovative, original writer, mother of the new experimental writers to follow, her chief weapons must be fashioned of language itself. Stein's deep concern with role and gender finds its focus in this play in an extended discussion of the power of naming. Will Anthony be able to preserve her own name? Will Indiana keep her name or take

Jo's? And what is the status of a woman like Henrietta M., who has no patriarchal marker at all?

> Let me present to you Henrietta M.
> it is rare in this troubled world
> to find a woman without a last name
> rare delicious and troubling. (67)

Susan B. Anthony, like Stein, is a woman who retains her own name, who has never married, never shared or diluted her identity. Despite Indiana Elliot's demands that she "choose a name" (and a husband), history has instead chosen Anthony and enshrined her in its cultural records. This status is visibly achieved in the play when the audience is allowed to admire a statue of Anthony.

Naming is tantamount to possessing. To establish himself, even the lowly Jo the Loiterer must claim a wife (54). In his male world, she is the object—women exist to be appropriated.

Jo the Loiterer	I want to tell oh hell.
	I want to tell about my wife.
Chris the Citizen	And have you got one.
Jo the Loiterer	No not one.
Chris the Citizen	Two then
Jo the Loiterer	No not two.
Chris	How many then
Jo the Loiterer	I haven't got one. (54)

Women are status symbols, emblems of value for those who have them.

During an "interlude," Anthony's meditation includes many of Stein's preoccupations, the issues of women who try to be powerful in the world: What is the value of politeness? Of soft over loud argument? What is the way to gain an audience? But for the men in the play, tradition and received form triumph over any attempt to establish a meaningful atmosphere for change. John Adams, for instance, thinks his family name is so important he cannot pay court to a woman he loves. If he had not been an Adams, then he would have kneeled at Constance Fletcher's feet and kissed her hand. Instead, he refrains, protecting both the present and the symbolic, dead father: "you would have ruined my father if I had had one" (62). The prohibition of the father, who "metaphorically says no to the child's desires" (Mitchell and Rose 1982, 16), functions despite his absence.

The maleness that Daniel and Leo Stein represent appears in many guises in the play, including that of God Himself. In Jo's account, Indiana plays Eve, source of all bitterness, who lays claim to a "tree" in his "garden" that is not hers; after the ensuing quarrel, both are expelled: "we took a train and we went where we went" (54). From that time forward, women like Angel More can either toil, "darn and wash and patch" (55), or rebel, punningly creating a new self, "Not any more. I am not a martyr anymore" (55). Susan B. Anthony's task, like Stein's, involves confronting and dispelling attitudes that seem as old as our civilization itself.

Daniel Webster, Anthony's chief antagonist, is the representative of masculine power and the structures of rationality and law that flow from it. Susan B. Anthony fears he "undertakes to overthrow her undertaking" (58), her program of personal and social liberation. While Anthony speaks of her impatience to have her reforms voted in, her need to protest, and her recognition of women's political needs, she is most of all concerned with their repressed interior state, their suppressed emotional lives, "who can bite their lips to avoid a swoon" (88). Webster, however, worries almost exclusively about exterior appearances, about institutions, about making points that please his compatriots, whose sexual and political preeminence is alluded to in Webster's reference to "the honorable member" (58). It can be said that Webster never sees the whole for its parts: "What interest . . . ," he wonders, "has South Carolina in a canal in Ohio" (58). His analytic style is reminiscent of Juliet MacCannell's description of the mindset of the Lacanian symbolic father, who reasons with "the discursive forms of knowledge and mastery" (MacCannell 1986, 78). How can he be expected then to understand Anthony's spiritual, ecstatic litanies when he speaks essentially another language? When Webster says things like "the harvest of neutrality had been great, but we had gathered it all," Anthony's reply is on an entirely different level:

> Near hours are made not by shade not by heat not by joy. . . . I enter into a tabernacle I was born a believer in peace, I say fight for the right, be a martyr and live, be a coward and die. . . . They leave us here. They come again. Don't forget they come again. (58)

The disempowered find it hard to make themselves heard while the Daniel Websters of the world command the floor. There is no simple solution for either Anthony or Stein. To allow "women to tell" (72), to decide not to be "one of two" (75), is to redefine the terms of our interactions by imagining ourselves and our speech anew; it is an act of birth and liberation.

Brothers: Identity Through Language

The processes of disguised autobiography that culminate in *Mother Of Us All* were present from the first in Stein's difficult texts. In *Two*,[3] a very early work (1910–1913) although it was not published until after Stein's death, she is already experimenting with shaping her text into a particular reflection of her evolving self-image as a lesbian and as an artist. The history of Stein's relationship with her brother Leo and her break with him in 1913, his moving out, and her creation of a separate household with Alice B. Toklas (who had been living at 27 rue de Fleurus since 1910), which concerned Stein throughout her life, is the central drama of this insular prose work.

From the beginning, Stein's work exhibits its characteristic focus on establishing the author's identity as a great artist, an important and independent person. In the way her words mesh, in disentangling them and separating the different strands of meaning from one another, Stein is able to present a covert analysis of her childhood sibling relationship and, by extension, of her adult social and romantic relationships:

> If one is one and one is not one
> of the two then is one and being one
> is not one of the two. . . . There were two. The two were he and she.
> She was one. He was one. There were two.
> There were he and she. (100)

The repetition[4] in *Two*, whether it proves intriguing or annoying to the reader, is central to Stein's rendering of the siblings' separation; confusion, backsliding, realliance, and further splintering seem to have formed the chief pattern: "more than once Leo tried to win back his sister's sympathy" (Simon, 107). In her narrative the words are forever duplicating, mirroring, and cancelling each other out until they finally go their own way for "her" and for "him." Wordsplitting and recombining help the "she" of *Two* to establish separate selfhood from the "he" who seeks to dominate her. Accepting this level of obscurity and repetition is the first and central test of any prospective reader. It is no accident that Leo's refusal to read such texts, his "ridiculing of her writing" (Simon, 105), is seen by Stein as an important part of the breakup with Leo: "It destroyed him for me and it destroyed me for him" (*Everybody's Autobiography* 1937, 77). Leo was certainly intolerant of his sister's aspirations; in a letter to the art collector Albert C. Barnes, he complains: "it's almost impossible to believe that she believes the stuff she wrote and equally difficult to believe she is lying" (Leo Stein 1950, 149).

But the degree of her early dependence on Leo, the act of will it must have taken to allow herself to face his disapproval and grow away from him, can be inferred by the humble image "she was the particle and the resemblance" (125)[5] that Stein invokes to describe their relationship. "There are not two of them," she declares in her opening, "there is one of them" (1). Years later, in *Everybody's Autobiography*, she would recall:

> He had always been my brother
> two years older and a brother.
> I had always been following. (75–76)

Two anticipates Stein's lifelong exploration of the unacceptable differences between man and woman, but it is also concerned with the specific differences between her brother and herself. A man's words, Leo's words, would engulf her in the masculine world; she has to find a communication that will not "inundate" (126) her. If Leo is logical, rational—he "estimates" and "concludes" (102), framing the experience, "leading, covering the time he was using" (98), which is her time as well—then she will fashion a language that is a rejection of the logical and its apparent antithesis. Despite Leo's attempts to control his sister, her language and life will slip away from him as she willfully creates an art and an identity that demonstrate and affirm her independence, the implied inner voice of the following passage:

> There was slipping sound sounding . . . she who in the midst was reflecting what was missing was not destroying that sound. (106)

"That sound" constitutes the characteristic "slippery" style of Stein's difficult texts. It allows her language a textural presence that is assertively nonlinear, nonlogical, unconfined to its textual mooring, unmale, un-Leo. In the present instance it involves using the repeated sounds of words as a distancing and reassuring technique for her separation from Leo. Mirroring with words will assure a safe break, one that can reject the old sibling relationship but keep the self intact.

The successful Leo, emblem of wholeness, is complete in himself. He never needs to think, or say, twice:

> He had the past and the present was there and he had the future . . . the decision . . . he had all that he had said . . . all that he had intended to have said. (106)

Even after her separation from Leo, however, Stein, no matter how idealized her guise or how insistent her claims to a similar spatial and temporal dominance, will remain "half":

> She was the time and the space and the place and the work and she was the whole and the half and the strength and the past. (134)

She chafes at his power and wishes for her own "way" to compete with his. His is the authoritarian principle that is not satisfied until its net encompasses the total territory; her situation parallels a rebellion against a hostile colonial presence:

> He did it all. He had the control of the half and he had the control of the whole. He had the complete way. (122)

How does the fragment achieve a fully realized status? The process is mysterious, like the process in nature by which a twin-containing egg splits into two identical parts. But for Stein, the writer, the essential ground and matter of this separation will be composed of language. The "he" hears "sound sounding" (105) but does not understand her voice because, unlike his, it reflects more than mere intellectual necessity: "he had not the sound . . . as pleasure in existing" (116). It is important to remember that Leo, whatever his spiritual and emotional condition, was actually becoming physically deaf at this point in his life (EA, 72–73.) His male physical power—"he was the one who had the thing" (117)—is enmeshed within his need to demonstrate mental acuity.[6] There seems to be no Leo at all apart from his ability to reason, elucidate, judge, decide, and direct (119–120). He organizes everything, including his sexuality: "He systematized every conception, he realized what was created . . ." (129).

If, in her celebration of her adult liberation, she must refuse her brother's hopes and expectations, his rejection of her must be emphatically developed, as in fact it actually was,[7] and so complete that there can be neither misunderstanding nor future hope of reconciliation:

> It was not in the lingering way that he used every day when he did say that he hoped they would stay away. (110)

Even during this rupture with Stein and Toklas, Leo remains aware, analytic, critical, decisive, cold, unforgiving, unreceptive to any explanations:

> He was the arbiter then. He saw the rest . . . he was not interested in all that there was to hear. (113)

It seems important for Stein to stress that it is Leo who makes a new, more equal, association impossible, even if the nature of Stein's new independence has not been overtly defined. "He did not consecrate what remained" (114). It does not appear to her that he will appreciate life alone—"he did not seem to enjoy the rest of what he had" (115)[8]— but will not seek a reconciliation: "he intended to remain away" (114).

Unlike the brother, the sister remains ambivalent, alternately hoping she has not hurt him and wondering if she should injure him more (118). She typically asks for forgiveness, not for her new behavior but for her old repressions and reticences: "pardon the only lady who was suppressing that feeling" (127). She begins slowly by listening (16) and speaking (17). She notices her growth and change (19) as she starts important work of her own (20). Developing this new inner strength, she passes through a period of suffering (20–21) to establish the nature of her need that will enable her to launch an attack (26) that will end in "succeeding in expressing" (37), "telling that she was knowing" (42), and "expressing receiving, mingling, loving and being" (48), leading to the highest ideal, "she is one being one" (53). Here she remakes and defines the whole, "she had learned to feel to be the whole of that . . . married . . . there was a union" (124–25). She is the "pleader" for a new lifestyle, not "apprehensive" any more, though "there was not any fashion" (125) for this new kind of relationship or for its open discussion in literature or life.

The achieved state of homosexual marriage, Gertrude Stein's clear but unspoken object, and the immediate cause of her problems with Leo, obtains notice in *Two* precisely because of the author's insistence that it remain directly unmentionable. Her future relations, both homosexual and literary, would prove to be as full of complexities, contradictions, and complications as was her previous relationship with Leo or her life as a single woman before she lived with him:

> Coming and not coming, enjoying and being charming, jerking and not jerking, gently and with enthusiasm, brutally and not completing, occasionally and continuing, steadily and explaining, excitedly and not decid-

ing . . . completing and repeating, repeating and denying . . . coming with
denying the coming. (7–8)

"She did not profit by learning the whole of a language when she had
the use of it all and said what she said" (117), Stein realizes. She is
destined to become the "pleader" of a secret cause, ever encumbered by
the dangers of disgrace, "poised" but disengaged. She must remember
that the "building" she now inhabits was "a copy of something" (134), a
now unspeakable past once shared with her brother, since every new
love partakes of the love of the past. In her difficult texts, Stein will
transform this past into an equally unspeakable present. What she has
done in separating from her brother is done, and it is "well done when
all the place was filled with that later feeling" (134), but the nature of
"that later feeling" remains remarkable for its lack of explicit definition.
Thus she is not being entirely candid when she writes that "she was the
one who spoke the thing that staying away from home meant everything" (108). The experimental style is founded on Stein's reluctance to
give "the thing" a name, even though it is "everything."

"A Complete Replacement of the Real Thing": A Glimpse of Stein's Interior Life in the Notebooks for *The Making Of Americans*

There is no single key to Stein's fierce ambivalences, her simultaneous need to both reveal and conceal her sexuality in her writing. As
Bridgman has written, "however euphemistic Gertrude Stein was
about sexual experience, it maintained its centrality in her work" (78).
But for readers familiar with the passionate multiple personae Stein
assumes in her literary works, her self-image in the folders of her
notebooks for *The Making Of Americans*, 1906–1908 (transcribed by
Leon Katz in the Gertrude Stein Collection at the Beinecke Library),[9]
suggests the tangle of powerful personal forces shaping her attitudes.
Together, the many speakers and voices of these notebooks offer a
compelling composite portrait of Gertrude Stein's interior life.

As the notebooks begin in 1906, Stein, at the age of 32, had been
living in Paris for three years, sharing her brother Leo's apartment at
27 rue de Fleurus, while also frequenting the artistic household of her
married, and eldest, brother Michael.[10] As a productive but unpublished writer (*Three Lives* would not be published until 1909, though
she had already finished a novel, *Things As They Are*, in 1903), and as a
collector of the new art and the new artists, a friend of Picasso, Braque,

Apollinaire, and Matisse, she had already developed her characteristic personal and literary styles. In 1907, she would first meet Alice B. Toklas, at Michael and Sarah Stein's home at 58 rue Madame, although she was not to live with her until 1910, finally causing Leo to move out, angrily, almost theatrically, in the fall of 1913. Her notebooks from this interesting period include a collection of possible material for her monumental *The Making Of Americans*—a trying-out of characters, scenes, and ideas for a novel that would not be published until 1925. More importantly, however, they are the intimate and frank diaries of an extraordinarily careful and subtle observer.

As might be expected, Stein's homosexual relationship with Alice B. Toklas is the central event of these notebooks. Stein's comments and observations reflect not only the lover's and the writer's perception of her role, but also include material seemingly recorded from the perspective of judging male family members. No matter what the narrative perspective, however, Stein almost always portrays herself as passive, a hostage self, fearing to be lost entirely or possessed only as an exquisite or freakish object, open to use or manipulation.

Stein discusses modes of defense of this beleaguered self, methods to escape injury. But even as she would protect her vulnerable self from exploitation by another, she is equally likely to join in the attack. Even more than the unpublished writings, the notebooks represent an entirely private communication; she feels free to call herself every name, from immoral to fat, as she rehearses her familiar disgrace: "You have no right to bring us up into a good position and then disgrace us" (12–15, Folder 4). Of course, she does not spare others, including Toklas, from an equally searching appraisal. Nearly all her wider social circle of salon friends are carefully dissected and catalogued, but her most bitter words are self-directed.

If sexuality plays the major role in the notebooks, it is nearly always accompanied by fears and defensive judgments. Sex is presented as being not merely potentially scandalous; it is seen as dirty, as polluting. Paradoxically, it must simultaneously be praised and valorized as the artist's energizing subject, indeed, the subject of all creativity. Whenever this contradiction threatens to become oppressive, Stein argues that art transcends both morality and consistency. Internal desire, not external physiology, determines true gender, or at least should, and the world of art is the world of should. Because art is transformational, the work of art cleanses experience: "Writing books is like washing hair. You got to soap it a lot of times before you start to rinse it" (C 27, Folder 1).

"Herman," as "her man," Stein's male identity, frequently meditates on her resemblance to particular men, from her brother to her
father to Picasso, and on her embodiment of male virtues, exploring
her distance from the traditional "feminine" norm, "adopting a male
persona against the feminine weakness to which her womanhood apparently consigned her" (Benstock 1986, 19). Thus, for instance, Stein
uses her own voice to observe, "I am just like my father" (2–5, Folder
1). Just as she magically transforms her gender to writing and in life,
she transforms her love relationship. Although she certainly considers
the relationship between herself and Alice B. Toklas to constitute a
form of imposture, it can, as art, be temporarily rendered into a mysti-
cal and sensual union that transcends and reshapes reality.

Her sexual situation, however, is never long allowed this level of
self-acceptance and idealization. While Stein's public self is usually
presented as powerful, and male, her private self always perceives its
vulnerability—Alice is the threatening one. Nothing is as simple as
Alice B. Toklas's famous image of "handmaiden to a great artist" might
suggest. In the notebooks, Stein shows Alice to be the strong one, the
aggressor, the proclaimer and enforcer of the most imperious demands.
Toklas is both the lady and the prostitute, with the latter office repre-
senting Toklas's "purer flame." The drama of the relationship of Stein
and Toklas, played out everywhere in the notebooks, echoes and mocks
Stein's public posture.

Stein's identity as an artist provides a substitute, a replacement for
the merely personal. It guarantees important change and redefines the
artist by connecting her to what is beautiful and ordered—"when
vulgarity flows together into a harmony, the thing you are and the
thing you would be" (6–16, Folder 1). In this way, "the thing you are"
might be controlled, masked, obliterated, even transmuted, by "the
thing you would be."

If Stein refuses direct narrative (1–19, Folder 1), her art, nonetheless, comes from a "genuine sensation" (11–9, Folder 2). It is not the art
but the world itself that is not "genuine." The best creative work will
be bound to the spirit. A true artist, like Matisse, could be obsessed by
the body, but he would "paint his soul at the end of his brush" (45, p.3,
Folder 2). If Picasso is Stein's type of the true creative genius, it is
because the intensity of his aesthetic, even more obviously than that of
Matisse, is allowed to transform actual experience, stretching its bor-
ders into areas that might be considered non-representational. In a
similiar vein, she praises her brother Leo for his scientific insight (45,

p.6, Folder 2) as offering yet another way to abstract and idealize the human experience. No wonder then the evident release manifest whenever Stein can assert that "aesthetic has become the whole of me" (14–7, Folder 3).

For Stein, true art must rival actual experience in being "exciting, sensual, reactive" (D 13–56, p.2, Folder 2). Everyone needs the idealization of beauty art provides, most especially the artist herself. Otherwise, "he can't sit still with his misfit inside him" (D 13–64, p.2, Folder 2). Better yet, the artist cannot be judged—she is outside morality, marginal, made differently from other women, with different means and aims, which can be conveniently explained by her status as artist.

If Toklas cannot create independently, it is because her reality is too "real" and acceptable to her. Toklas's personality was more suited to "the service business, the giving people what they wanted, the humility, adoration of idols, higher life, aesthetics, music that was all the pride side, academic learning . . . (46, p.5, Folder 2). Toklas's satisfaction with her world is a sign she lacks "sufficient egotism" (C 17, Folder 6). Stein, however, cannot create without her help. Paradoxically, the creators, alienated from the "real" world, may need the helpers more than the helpers need them.[11]

If Stein's public self continuously proclaims "sufficient egotism," the other voices of these journals admit her search for "the ultimate dependence" (11–3, Folder 4). If Stein's art is based on her personal liberation, the energy to observe is strangely catalyzed through possession by another.

As is well known, Stein ultimately chose to live privately as a man and to think and write of herself in those terms. Without forgetting the enormous difficulty of being an independent woman and artist in the first decades of this century, readers of the notebooks will be shocked and saddened by the intensity of Stein's self-hatred. More surprisingly, perhaps, Stein's attitude extends to include other people, particularly women, particularly Toklas, who would remain Stein's closest associate for most of her adult life. In her rejecting and judgmental attitude toward Toklas, Stein projects her own guilty sexual feelings, assigning Toklas the role of the immoral temptress: "She is pretty nearly all bad" (C 31, p.2, Folder 2).

As an artist, Stein makes something beautiful out of something she considers, at least much of the time, to be essentially ugly. As a substitute for reality, the aestheticized object is the gateway to a world the imposter would normally be barred from.[12] As traditional gender is disarticulated in the fusion of reality and fantasy, so too are Stein's grammatical forms. Her universe is taken to the extreme limits of plasticity, as her homosexuality erodes traditional social and verbal boundaries.

The displacements and metamorphoses we see in Stein's texts continually validate the perceived lawlessness of her emotions. Stein, whether identifying with her irascible and somewhat frightening father or rejecting the logical and intellectual world of her brother Leo, is ever conscious of her subversion of the order of nature. Art is the replacement for the world, satisfying the passion to penetrate the secret, the riddle, of her magic identification with the male universe.[13] Once in the sphere of magical achievement, she becomes the subject for further transformations. As Chasseguet-Smirgel (1984) writes, "art palliates the defects of nature" (96) but "the opposite bears the indelible expression of that which it negates" (98).

If Stein, expectedly, concentrates on her own condition in these notebooks, her relationship to her father is often the basis of her self-image. She exults in her male anger—"I do it too, just like my father" (2–5, Folder 1)—but she also ruefully complains about inheritance: "it's hard living down the tempers we are born with" (1–11, Folder 1). Her male persona is linked to the doing of great things, as she tries to explain to someone she names in parentheses "Leon," likely to be her brother Leo, but perhaps alternatively or simultaneously Leon Solomons, a fellow student Stein was sexually attracted to who died from cancer in 1900 (Bridgman 29).

Later in the same section she compares her intellect to her brother/lover Leo/Leon: "Leon like me in ideas and revolt" (2–24, Folder 1). However, the brother with whom she was "strong in love and worship" (6–21, Folder 1) would gradually be replaced by the male persona she harbored, "the misfit inside her" (D 13–64, p.2, Folder 2). Her assumption of a male identity will encourage other women "with the real stuff" in them; even though they are "made different" from men (11–2, Folder 2), they can assume equally powerful roles and identities.

Admired people have "real stuff" or "the real thing" inside them, but this supposed reality, Stein is always discovering, is more than likely itself suspect, meretricious, an imposition, a masquerade. She speaks of a friend, Penelope, who is better because in her there is "almost a complete replacement of the real thing" (D 13–52, p.3,

Folder 2). In the same passage she hints that this "replacement" comes about as a result of an "injury" that creates "an autocratic queen" (the word *king* is crossed out in the manuscript) "who can do no wrong" (51, Folder 2).

She puts women into other categories from which she carefully distinguishes herself. The feminine type she calls "Dolene": "good-natured, sweet . . . sympathetic, motherly, never get tired, etc. . . . sweetness and humanity, it's not me" (C-18, Folder 3). She identifies with "the Scandinavian dramatist," probably Strindberg, "whose fear of feminization . . . caused his death" (6–11, Folder 1). Womanliness may be admired in others but she does not emulate the ideal. Her sexuality is "masculine, aggressive, concentrated to attack, not attract" (30, Folder 3). She seems strong like a man, but yet she wants to take on a passive, womanly approach to a strong partner. She senses her own divided nature: ". . . rarely favorite with men; often men mistake in women like myself because my temperament and point of view, intellect and consciousness is masculine and the erotic emotion is masculine that the sexual nature is, my actual sexual nature is pure servant female. I find it difficult to work up energy enough to dominate" (L-30, Folder 3).

Does Stein mean by this that, in disguising her true sexuality, she wants both the advantage of aggression and the social acceptance of passivity? Although she sees its social advantages, the stereotyped feminine ideal does not appeal to her: "Lord deliver us from sweet little women" (2–15, Folder 4). Her homosexuality may reverse and mix traditional roles, but it still employs them. "As a lesbian, her relationship with Alice Toklas duplicated the imbalance apparent in many heterosexual unions" (Benstock 1986, 18).

Stein's male identification can cause her to assume a grandiose persona. In her early relationship with Toklas, she is never satisfied by the attention she is given and compares Toklas unfavorably with other women who "have it in them to really love a man because he is great . . . Alice don't" (C-26, Folder 6). Stein wants choiceless, nonjudgmental love in her relation with Toklas—a childlike wish. Ironically, even as Stein speaks of women as "amiable children" she wishes for infallibility for herself (I-3, Folder 8).

This is not to say Stein is unaware of the ability of certain women, Toklas in particular, to manipulate her emotionally. An exasperating aspect of her male identity is Alice's propensity to call her bluff and treat her like a man—to handle her with the special disrespect she reserves for aged male dinner partners, for example: "She can make you talk like one of her old gentlemen to whom she loves to listen and be docile to and so she makes a poor thing of one because one talks badly then, she listens . . . but she owns you" (D 56, p.4, Folder 2). This theme of ownership comes back again and again as Stein explores the meaning of her relationship with Toklas, much as it had in her consideration of her relationship with Leo.

Stein fears that because Toklas is not creative in the same way she herself is, she wants to bask in Stein's success and be creative by association. But this lessens the power of the artist herself: "Gradually she gets superior . . . by appropriating your work and so pulling you down to [her] level" (46, Folder 2). Even Stein cannot give Toklas everything she needs—she must seek out others as well for "real experience, a sensation of beauty, higher life, aesthetics" (46, p.6, Folder 2). Stein, on the other hand, affirms her own experience through art (43, p.2, Folder 2).

It is not Toklas's lack of originality that creates her passion for ideas—Stein's harsh estimate is that, like some other women, Toklas is not "the real thing. She replaces the lack of her own imagination with a manufactured article . . . she wants to be it . . . to know the beauty of power" (MA-49, Folder 4). So she "subdues" Stein, the "one she needs for loving" (C-26, Folder 6). Stein is Toklas's way of "connecting on to . . . the clever people" (D-24, Folder 7).

But with Stein as the focus of Toklas's affective and aesthetic life, the "connection" between them can chafe the independent artist. Toklas grasps at Stein with a jealous fervor that makes other relationships difficult, such as the one with Annette Rosenshine.[14] Concerning the "Annette business," Stein remarks that Toklas "cares more about loving than about me, that is, she cares more about having complete possession of loving me than of loving me, in short, the perfect emotion is more to her than the object of it" (H-8, Folder 7). Stein fears this total possession just as she is conscious of, and suspicious of, similiar attempts by her brother Leo and her father. Stein muses about "the drama between Alice and me, me wanting to give yet resisting being owned, wanting the feeling of generosity but not wanting to be possessed" (I-3, Folder 8).

Toklas's demands for loyalty and commitment make Stein fearful of her dependency. Stein's ambivalence about her is continuous and obvious. It may be that by criticizing Toklas as morally reprehensible, Stein can allay her guilt over the source of her own sexual feelings, transferring her fear of self to fear of Toklas, making her appear as the "dirty one." But as we see throughout her writings, Stein draws the very thinnest of lines between aversion and fascination.

Stein presents Toklas's sexuality and even her gender as radically different from her own. Stein's image of Toklas resembles nothing else so much as a nineteenth-century male stereotype of women, down to the "mother/whore" dichotomy. Stein speaks of Toklas's divided feminine nature as "not dangerous, not effective, no evil intention, no steadfast attention of any sort" (D 13–56, Folder 2). Her attribution of "lowness" to Toklas's intrinsic feminine nature sounds like the worst misogyny about a woman being a benighted soul, having "no intention to be low, no struggle, no moral nature, in the sense of effort. To be low . . . is beauty to her" (D 13–56, p.2, Folder 2).

If Toklas is "low," she must make Stein "high"—put her on a pedestal and make her into an "idol" (D 13–56, p.3, Folder 2). Toklas must have someone to look up to—her ideals, like those of a childhood innocent, convince her she really "wants to be good" (D 13–56, p.3, Folder 2), but her "flavor esthetic" (D 13–56, p.4) requires the stimulation of emotional and aesthetic objects and people. This idea of "flavor esthetic" is part of Stein's special vocabulary for typing people, one she created during her studies with William James. Stein seems to mean by it a strongly sexual person who prefers direct experience to abstract thought. Toklas then is a sort of anti-Leo whose longing for experience, her "flavor character," constitutes her central damning trait.

But because Toklas grasps onto Stein as an "idol" to transcend her own "lowness," the idol, too, is dragged down and becomes "the idol with the feet of clay" (46, Folder 2). Stein feels unappreciated, a potential sacrifice to placate Toklas for her missing creative powers: "You are hers, then, submissive, docile, stupid, humble, as she is then to you and so you are dead and she passes over your dead body" (46, Folder 2).

Toklas resembles the other women in Stein's circle in that all are presented as suspect. In this intensely private handwritten source (her later works were transcribed by Toklas), Stein vents her worst suspicions about Toklas as a model for women in general, a nature to be made up of "every conceivable kind of weakness, crookedness, laziness, stupidity . . . the evasive female" (46, p.3, Folder 2). Even Toklas's affinity to the world of artists and objects of art, while judged "worthwhile," is also vulgar (46, p.5, Folder 2). She decides that a friend, identified only as Neith, has the same basic personality type as Toklas. Both are of the "servant girl" type, "sale dirty, wallows in filth" (C-15, Folder 3). This

association between servants and sexuality in Stein's mind is reminiscent of the kind of pornographic fantasy of oppression that finds servants to be both sexually available and morally unreliable. Even more
strangely, however, Stein also sees herself, for whom "point of view,
intellect, consciousness is masculine, and the erotic is masculine" (C 30,
Folder 3), as a "servant type" (C 30, Folder 3).

"Put Language In The Waist": The Critique of Women in *Geography and Plays*

The war that drove Gertrude Stein and Alice Toklas from Paris to
Majorca from 1915 to 1916 also turned Stein into a more self-accepting
and sympathetic observer of women. As Stein grew more dependent
on Alice Toklas for companionship, Toklas's activities became of necessity more of a subject for Stein's writing. Keeping largely in the company of women, her writings of this time still typically contain extended critical discussions of women's sexuality and identity, but with
more humor and less apparent bitterness, especially since this material
is presented from the implied perspective of homosexual romance. As
Bridgman has noted, "One sign of her incipient reconciliation to her
private vision came when she confessed that she preferred to write
about women. 'It is clearer . . . I know it better, a little, not very much
better' " (78).

In *Geography and Plays* (1922), a collection of short plays written
during her Majorcan exile, 1915–16, Stein offers a radical public critique of women that in many ways builds on the observations of her
earlier notebooks. Instead of their too-customary pursuits of narcissism
and authoritarian obedience, Stein argues that women need to liberate
themselves from shame, false romantic aspirations, bodily weaknesses,
and traditional roles. She urges women to break out of enclosures,
whether house forms, clothing forms, legal forms, or social forms. She
implies that ideal marriage, unrestrained and unlicensed, can occur
only between women, because there is no basis for a connection between the "logical man," modelled on Leo, and the "intuitive woman,"
modelled on Stein.

If Stein's theoretical ideal for sexual relationships between women
combines traditional and radical assumptions, this reflects the actual
state of affairs in the Stein-Toklas household. Despite Stein's commitment to a reimagining of existing mores, she nonetheless adapted traditional sexual roles in her relationship with Toklas. "Stein wrote and slept

while Toklas cooked, embroidered, and typed" (Cook 730). For Stein, though perhaps with less sharpness than earlier in her life, primary relationships would always be caught up in an uncomfortable ambivalence, an essential disquiet that radiates across her difficult texts.

Sexuality is a source of creative self-expression and of pride, but it also continues to constitute a threat. Her pride in her independent choices is always balanced by her fears of disclosure, condemnation, and abandonment. This doubleness, here as elsewhere, has extensive stylistic and narrative implications. In *Geography and Plays*, although the ideas presented are very much Stein's own and the tonalities controlled for ironic effect, the plays present themselves as being composed entirely of conversations overheard.

Every play has as its focus another aspect of feminine life. If one is married, are there also a large wardrobe, children, and rivals? Can orders be refused? Is the woman's relationship with her husband or her lover based on fantasy or fact? Concern with personal appearance, particularly youthfulness, facial beauty, and clothing, is a thread that links the plays together. Women, seen only in the context of social interaction, become objects of appraisal (and exchange) by others. Mrs. Marchand closes one of Stein's typical estimates, "Please Do Not Suffer," with the cynical observation that:

I have met her. She is very pleasant. I did not think she was his wife. I thought she was his daughter. So did we all. (266)

Mrs. Marchand, a writer like Stein, has promised to take notes when a man pays attention to a woman.

Much of Stein's observation of married couples developed from regular at-homes, afternoons and evenings of gossip over food. Although Alice Toklas is admirably well-suited to this milieu, she is also taken for granted as cook, housekeeper, secretary—a type of the traditional "good" wife Stein is quick to criticize in a heterosexual context. Nevertheless, it is undoubtedly true that sexual dominance in the one and submission in the other dictated the actual performance of menial tasks in the Stein-Toklas household. Expectably then, Gertrude's continuing dependence fostered a mixture of gratitude for and mistrust of Alice's nurturing role.

Alice's world as presented in these plays seems a small and comfortable place, a world of women, cooking, gardening, knitting, talking, and worrying about love. The plays express these concerns in a synesthesia of food, clothing and sensuality, body- and house-parts.

That the subject of *Geography and Plays* should be "the physical attributes and behavior of women" (Bridgman 144) is a predictable innova-
tion for Gertrude Stein's theater, but she balances these conventions of
domesticity with a radical narrative structure that avoids any direct
mention of homosexuality, its central thematic preoccupation, while
also dispensing with stage directions, the routine allocation of speeches
to specific characters, conventional "plot development," and transi-
tions between acts and scenes. These techniques allow the playwright
to present the factual, trivial, and mundane material in ways that
further disguise, but do not repress, her forbidden and intimate erotic
concerns. Later chapters of this book gloss a selection of the bawdy
references in *Geography and Plays*, and of other works, in their many
modulations. Stein's particular talent for parody and word-play makes
her text rich with possibilities, displaying several hierarchical and contradictory levels of meaning.

Stein has a double objective in the presentation of her sexuality in
her difficult texts. Her first need is to reveal her feelings and to defend
herself against conventional ideas about "romance" and sexual roles in
general. In "Ladies Voices," "White Wines," "For the Country Entirely," "Every Afternoon," "Please Do Not Suffer," "Counting Her
Dresses," and "If You Had Three Husbands," for instance, Stein's
considerable powers of social observation and her use of herself as a
yardstick for measuring the liberation of other women provide valuable
illustrations of what she saw as debilitating stereotypes. Her second
need, however, is to mask her erotic material, especially her use of
disguised autobiography, to allow it to seem a sort of innocent and
elegant nonsense.

It is not simply that she knows each side of the sexual equation
firsthand and that she is sufficiently distanced from both male and
female to allow for skepticism. For instance, in "If You Had Three
Husbands," one feminine voice admits, "It pleased me to say that I was
pretty" (386), while another, of undefined sex, asserts, "She pleased me
for Eye saw" (387). A masculine counterpart responds a little later,
"Call me handsome" (389). There is an obsessive preoccupation with
body images, "Why need I be seen?" (389), until the description of
dress becomes instead a metaphor of concealment, serving chiefly to
emphasize the body hidden underneath. This seems certainly to be the
case in "White Wines," whose "masked balls" (204) and "old chink"
(211) cannot be changed by the relentless piling on of garments symbolic of either one sex or the other.

In "Counting Her Dresses" the clothes must be cleaned, collected, counted, catalogued, managed (284), even while the speaker polishes furniture. Stein's alliteration helps to reinforce the ludicrous effect of wardrobe phobia. Her characters remind others in this play that "I want a cloak" (276), and "we need clothes. And wool. And gloves. And waterproofs" (280). They even argue about whether these are necessities: "I do not mention clothes. No you didn't but I do" (282). The dress itself may not explain everything about the woman inside it: "We saw a dress. We saw a man" (283). "If You Had Three Husbands" promises, in the section "Present Homes," that "I will never mention an ugly skirt"; and in the section "Their end" states flatly, "I don't like to be fitted" (386, 390). The concept of being fitted into clothing molds contrasts with such a basic approach to bodily knowledge as "sitting comfortably" (279). Vapid and sophisticated coverings, culturally imposed, are exchanged for the body's natural expressiveness, the delights of the tongue, the loins, and the bosom. "Put . . . language in the waist" (211), Stein urges.

The world of allusive equivalences is equally present in another familiar feminine activity, the preparation of food. Everything concerned with cooking takes priority in *Geography and Plays*. But when a "spoon" in "White Wines" becomes both a "touching" and "golden" reminder of romantic love, Stein rebels. Detesting this kind of genteel approach to physical needs, she instead advises readers to "show the tongue strongly in eating" (210). The identification of eating with sexuality becomes more apparent in a section where body parts mingle with culinary meditations:

Butter . . . why is a loin large . . . there is no cake in front.

. . . .

An army of invincible and ever ready moustaches

. . . .

A moon . . . and little bits of eels in a special sauce

. . . .

Why should there be solemn cuppings . . . (211–213)

This imagery suggests that sexual appetite be accepted in the same way as food, but the speaker always refrains from direct statement. Stein does not expect her readers to be blind to the implications of this imagery. Four other characters in "For the Country Entirely," Mr. and Mrs. Eaton and Mr. and Mrs. Beef, give an impression of vulgarity in a fusion of sexuality, food, and marriage. Genevieve announces in "Please Do Not Suffer" that although she was ruined by a butcher she continues to eat meat. Alice Toklas's nurturing function in her relationship with Stein is symbolized by a cow,[15] and so the chorus in "Counting Her Dresses" is thankful for the cow. Characteristically, Stein purposefully convolutes her meaning, taking the opposite point of view as well—the nurturer requires someone to accept the favor. "Can you be thankful. For what. For me" (277). This complex metaphorical style serves as an obfuscation, at times reducing the forbidden to nearly perfect banality.

Shopping at "cunning and cheap" sales, dusting and redusting in "White Wines," gardening and sewing in "Every Afternoon" are all seen as stereotypical activities of an "other," one half of a couple constituted of a writer and a buyer, or a reader and a knitter. Genevieve has to have her daughter's coat made twice and sleeps from boredom, while Mrs. Marchand has to excuse herself to "give my baby his luncheon" in "Please Do Not Suffer." The refrain "come to sing and sit" from "Counting Her Dresses" (276) further stylizes and disguises the erotic motif of these plays, allowing the hospitable "come" and "when will you come" to be repeated so often they become a sort of ornamental litany.

Two voices in "For the Country Entirely" discuss precisely this question: Why is it necessary to be, like Mrs. Cryst, "discreet and timid" (234)? (The name *Mrs. Cryst* itself seems to emphasize the use of indirect narrative techniques such as the parable.) In an old-fashioned, epistolary style, the hostess, addressing a Mr. King, probes for the correct attitude: "I have no means of satisfying myself whether I am obliged to be careful or not." He asks, "Careful of what," and the hostess replies, "Of what I say in public" (235). Even "good news" must be carefully presented. The voices in "Every Afternoon," the title of which implies a continual open house, discuss their affairs and those of others with the same veiled and knowingly guarded innuendoes that must often have been heard in Stein's salon:

> Were you expecting something.
> I don't know.
> Don't you know about it at all.
> You know I don't believe it.
> She did.
> Well they are different.
> I am not very careful. (256)

There are irritable rejoinders—"Don't say you haven't been told . . . very well then explain . . . yes and I will not cry" (257)—which remind the audience that this is a play primarily about a lesbian romance whose disagreements, pleasures, and optimism parody the idea of perfect union. The tea-party crowd and the couple alternate until finally one lover introduces the other to the group: "I am proud of her." Someone in the room responds, "You have every reason to be and she takes it so naturally." The lover reasserts, "It is better that it is her hands," and the group accepts, imitating a marriage ceremony with "Yes of course" (258).

The idea of homosexual marriage will be extended further, as an idealized feature of the Stein-Toklas relationship, but romantic love in these plays has to do mostly with aggression, with who holds power in the relationship. Love itself appears splintered into all its guises, from the mockingly bland to the profoundly sincere and even lachrymose. The section "House to House," when read to suggest "body to body" in "White Wines," has a mysterious stubborn "habit" that always remains the same:

> Not left by always screaming . . . made quiet, quite quiet . . . refuses all chances to change . . . that cut in two . . . which credited a long touch . . . which made darkness bitter and clanging . . . which has the best situation . . . cautious and serious and strange and violent and even a little disturbed . . . better than almost anything . . . so little irritating, so wondering and so unlikely is not more difficult than every other. (213)

This, about as complete a statement about sexual love as is allowed anywhere in *Geography and Plays*, presents an interesting fractioning of Gertrude Stein's attitudes. Her reaction to her own emotions is complex and defensive; something frightening and blameworthy resists her insistence that hers is the best of all possible loves and no harder to sustain than others.

On the other hand, the suffocatingly close atmosphere of intimacy in "Every Afternoon" clearly demonstrates the attributes of heterosexuality Gertrude Stein disliked, the relationships in which people are not only "hopeful and pleased" (254) and "equally pleased" (255) but, in addition, "easily deceived" and "rude." A lover uselessly laments "he was so necessary to me" (255). As the voices echo "happy" and "content," an eerie *Happy Days* results, prefiguring Beckett by several decades. Marriage, in "Please Do Not Suffer," is what prevents Mrs. Marchand from traveling, "because my husband cannot go away" (264). Besides its limitations, marriage also has an unnerving tendency to duplicate: Count Daisy Wrangle's Danish friend was married to "four different men" as well as being a "good friend to each one of them" (263). Legal marriage seems to have inherent in its structure a fantasy of deception no less than homosexual marriage.

> Can you laugh at me.
> And then say.
> Married.
> Yes. (280)

But if the lesbian style is defended as advantageous, it is done only indirectly. "Fixed" but not "licensed" (380), the couple in "If You Had Three Husbands" is not tempted to legalize and strangle the bond with forms. Being "naturally married" has as much to do with "likeness to loving" (380) or the comfortable sameness of the female body as with "not signing papers or anything" (378). The homosexual "choice" so frequently mentioned is not an openly debated subject as much as an implicitly assumed *fait accompli*: "Out from the whole wide world he chose her" (379).

Despite Stein's assertions of emotional security, a palpable disquiet remains: In "Every Afternoon," the speaker discourages reflection: "if you remember, you will remember other things that frighten you" (258). Advice in "Counting Her Dresses" contrasts the "careful obedient industrious" image of a woman with the spontaneous rebel: "Act quickly. Do not mind the tooth" (275–76). Elsewhere, an anxious mother wants her daughter to be "polite" (379). There is no direct explanation offered as to why the plaintive associations of romantic love, fainting and nerves, are devalued, while the male virtues often associated with war and battle are highly praised.

Alice B. Toklas, the focusing subject of these plays, must perform an ambiguous double role, incorporating the perfection of traditional womanhood with the achievement of Stein's sexual liberation. This contradictory status, like the hesitancy at the center of Stein's boldest assertions, typifies the dilemmas of Stein's position. Stein is a connoisseur of such complexities. As she demonstrated when she wrote Toklas's "autobiography," Stein can appreciate the limitations of the stereotype Toklas represents even as she celebrates what is valuable and personally useful in that stereotype.

Stein affirms deep emotional attachments, but only those that support selfhood and do not subordinate character to house forms (doors, walls, windows, furniture), to clothing (dresses, corsets, jackets, hats, feathers, gloves, waterproofs), or to meretricious legal formalities (licenses, papers, wills). Instead Stein demands "a complete actual present" (Mellow 306), a release from archaic attitudes and superficial gentility. The instincts are to be trusted more than learned responses: "Do not refuse to be wild" (390). But the homosexual nature of these instincts is never clarified. Stein merely urges women to infuse their behavior with the vigor and dominance characteristically thought of as male prerogatives, and to counteract the passive and withdrawn syndrome associated with femininity. In her recognition of spiritual equality between partners, her dislike of imposed roles, her acceptance of lust, and her fusion of aggressive and nurturing concepts of love, Gertrude Stein re-evaluated mores defining sexual behavior. The express realization of these judgments in lesbian romance, however, remains a forbidden topic, to be approached only with the greatest caution.

2

"Is Flesh Advisable?"
The Interior Theater of
Gertrude Stein

For many of the lyrical and revealing pieces from her early work, "Painted Lace" (PL), written in 1914; "Pink Melon Joy" (GP), "Possessive Case" (AFAM), and "No" (AFAM), all written in 1915; "Lifting Belly" (BTV), written in 1917; and "Not a Hole" (BTV) and "A Sonatina Followed by Another" (BTV), both written in 1921, Stein invented a witty code that played upon the details of her sexual and domestic self. In such a private autobiographical style she can tell everything—and she does. The works also have inherent literary qualities that would make them worthy of notice even if they did not reveal so much of the author's personality and habits. They speak in her private but authentic voice—warm, teasing, with exaggerated flights of fancy and whimsy that point to the more radical developments of her later years. The subject and style are, then, both testing grounds; in a sense, her life would become her art. Erotic, subconscious elements are allowed to interact with conscious craft to produce documents of the interior life.

In this "secret autobiography," centrally concerned with sex and sexual attitudes, Stein moves easily from her characterizations of society's vision of homosexuality to her parody of this vision, from her romantic situation to a frank appraisal of her body, from trite lovemaking words to passionate emotions to pure, playful nonsense, attempting to deal with all the worlds and acts of love. Stein invents words for Alice B. Toklas, for the female sexual organs, and for the forms of sexual caress. Intentional elements are interspersed with the spontaneous expressions that rise to her mind as she writes—the inner "automatic" spirit of her art.

In her poetic recreation of her love relationship with Toklas, Stein has a remarkable array of technical possibilities at her disposal, some already tested in other works preoccupied by the senses, such as "Melanctha" and *Q.E.D.* In her repetitions, mimicking, role playing as "author," Stein has always tried on attitudes like hats in front of the bedroom mirror. She creates a magic theater, in which she plays actor and audience at once. Her attitudes surface and change, coalesce and fragment. If at first she seems to affirm her passion, later she questions and mocks, even denies the worth and quality of her relationship.[1] Autobiographical themes of identity, self-justification, narcissism, and pride occupy her as well as moral questions of guilt, innocence, sin, security, and risk, and all of these are juxtaposed with frank homosexual statements and naive, totally positive images of her relationship. She finally seasons her text lightly with a straight-faced romantic vocabulary that might in other contexts pass for heterosexual.

For Gertrude Stein, identity or role playing is central to her "marriage" with Alice Toklas. "Painted Lace" gives the couple a "title" that must be lived up to: "Richly was the title deserved. They did it . . . they spent hours" (PL, 1). The defiant tone is eased by an important subterfuge of Stein's: the use of the impersonal "it" or "that" to replace "vagina" or "intercourse" or to refer to other sexual ideas. Her more bohemian impulses are thus balanced by a streak of the puritanical, and she is anxious enough about sex to make its discussion essential to her writing during several phases of her career. She needs to distance the facts of her personal life so that she may examine and reapproach them. Indeed, when Stein deals with identity, it must become theatrical.

In "A Sonatina Followed by Another," Stein assumes the persona of a "singer," with Toklas as her exotic muse, her "little Jew" (BTV, 1). Using a reductionist logic, Toklas takes on the identity of "Godiva." Although worshipped, Toklas is denigrated into a fantasy figure, a muse, but also a "mistress" (4), a forbidden consort. Only these images have the power to arouse the sexuality of the writer. Toklas pleases in the subordinate position, "as an apprentice" (8) to a great man,[2] Caesar or Seneca, or a Gertrude Stein, who "loved to be wed" (16) and demands to be cherished.

Toklas's submissive work, to "make dresses, knit and sew," takes on a different character when her cooking can be "to make that fire" ("No" AFAM, 60). In this passage, as in many others in "No," Stein speaks with Toklas's voice. Deliberately juxtaposing bedroom and kitchen, Toklas's personality, "cordial, liked by everybody" ("No," 68), functions as an aspect of her willingness to serve, to be "easily ordered about." Toklas has many roles; Stein's assumption of mastery makes Toklas's "wifely" role possible in all its dimensions: being friendly, liked, at her husband's disposal, and passionate. Even Toklas's negative aspects are subject to double vision: her negatives become positives, her nervousness comes from being "anxious to please me" ("No," 68); her obedience makes her Stein's "child." In the absence of prescribed roles, Stein both reinvents the traditional ones and finds new ones.

As has been discovered by many commentators, "Lifting Belly" is literally composed as the act of lovemaking; identity is buried in the act and any reflections outside of it seem superfluous. Yet the lovers are closely described, one "fierce and tender" (BTV, 66), the other "sister" (77) and not "mistress" (82). A masterful Caesar can still be kind, even if the role of the lover becomes a "duty" (89) and an "obligation" (75) to be fulfilled. As lovers, Stein and Toklas act too flagrantly, "making a spectacle" (90) in the eyes of the world. But when she probes beyond the mores of courtship and styles of lovemaking, Stein can still ask questions of the deepest import: "What is a man? What is a woman?" (93). Stein underscores her belief that these roles exist mainly as they are expected and demanded. They are enacted, dramatized, drawn out of one another.

As "Lifting Belly" concentrates more on the act itself and not on the characters performing it, "Possessive Case" focuses almost entirely on the identity of the "man." His sexual activity, his appearance and personality are the subjects for discussion. His lovemaking is rational: "I measured a sister" (AFAM, 112), "a thin lady asleep" (113). The relationship could be thought of as a house where the two of them live, but since it is an unexpected pairing, their house is "not mentioned anywhere" (119). This piece brings up the subject of sex roles so as to speak against them. The persona shows a characteristic ambivalence in both wanting to be one of the fathers (to resemble one's own father [122]), but rejecting all the trappings of the father's role: refusing to "plead moustaches" (159).

Guilt and justification, important for Stein's writing, are also aspects of her relationship with Toklas. Their treatment of each other grows out of their concepts of sexual roles. First, Stein presents the facts of her situation as questions. When she repeats them, they become assertions, affirmations. She demands, then retracts; she confesses and flaunts. She clearly recognizes the existence of guilt in her relationship with Alice but finds as many ways of supporting her mode and justifying her style: nature, her appetites, the inherent goodness of her mate, what is necessary and unavoidable. Pushed on by her feelings of guilt, she undermines reality the better to reconstruct it. She establishes the boundaries only to gain the satisfaction of straying beyond them.

In her humorous "mixed" manner, Stein tries to say and to be in many ways at once, including her ambivalence about values and embedding that ambivalence in her meanings. If she speaks of sex as a "ride" (a common slang designation) she does so with a double perspective: "No better hidden feelings. During one of their rides there was no objection" ("Painted Lace," 3). The feelings are "better," enjoyable, but of necessity "hidden." The possibility of objection is both endlessly brooded on and airily dismissed. To love where there might be objection is risky, but this, of course, is a great encouragement. Stein's persona refuses shame, calls her lover's body the best ("No," 41), speaks of their satisfaction (43), denies regret (45), and recalls the sorrow of loneliness.

The problems of guilt and certainty are also fundamentally reflected in her attitudes toward her art:

Lifting belly pencils to me.
And pens. ("Lifting Belly," 88–89)

She answers the charge of pornography, concluding that homoerotic love is "not naughty," and "I want to go on . . . I want a narrative based on that" ("No," 46). Though she claims that her love does not need justification, she posits a "defense of boxes" (49). She makes lovemaking more real through telling, "to have my wife hear" ("A Sonatina Followed by Another," 28) that it is "very pleasant to be wedded" (30). Not the least of the love's attributes, its power to inspire, derives from both its forbidden and its absurd elements.

As Stein can move from the equality of sisterhood to hierarchical concepts of the roles of husbands and wives, she also changes from the neutral, analytical tone of "adjusted" (8) to the superstitious, dirty/clean dichotomy to discuss homosexual love. She anticipates every facet of the world's view, and its opinions are delivered in a good-humored, rhyming mode by a sympathetic persona. In front of a disapproving society, it is "come dirty me . . . I am for thee" (8). In this work, her technique is to condense the two feelings—first the public image, then a romanticized version of that image. Her recognition of the public part of herself that thinks of her sexuality as "dirty" must be concealed by a fantasy of acceptance. To argue for this, she boasts: "We are a model to everyone. We are wonderfully productive" (8). To disarm the traditional morality of others, she adopts a moralistic tone, parodying religious belief, the narrator speaking of "reform for two" and the need to "atone." As in "I atone with smiles and miles" (15), however, deliberate humor undercuts the idea of sinfulness. The couple's very shapes are pleasing: "I couldn't imagine gladder or more perfect shapes" ("Pink Melon Joy" GP, 360). Questioning and doubt establish a rhetorical situation in which she cannot only ask questions, and answer them, but also raise further questions. By this process she extends the complexities of her inquiries and emphasizes the relativity of all judgments and values.

Because marriage is a social institution, the way "she" relates to the narrator's associates is important. Often "she" and the sexual act are talked about in front of friends, argued for and complimented, made public, as if the act had metamorphosed into the lover herself: "Lifting belly . . . a credit to me . . . an occasion to please me . . . courteous . . . hilarious, gay and favorable" ("Lifting Belly," 71). At other times, the lover-wife is only an adequate entertainment (73). Occasionally, a note of anger enters, and the self-justification seems directed at enemies: "I have done as I wished and I do not feel any responsibility to you" (78). Yet she can also articulate the "outside" audience's reaction when she speaks of reforming.

Frequently in "Lifting Belly" self-praise and blame move past mere self-justification to forge a "rhetoric of marriage," in which all the other voices are overwhelmed by a string of approving superlatives. Not only are "wishes fulfilled," the couple "bathing in bliss" (86), but even adjectives suggestive of wedding presents (and social acceptance) crop up, along with the necessary congratulations: "I congratulate you in being respectable and respectably married" (90). Lifting belly, the act of love, constitutes the complete family experience, including brother, father, and married couple, "lifting belly names it" (95). Of what occurs privately between the married couple, her tone is slangy, mockingly dismissive: "No need of regretting a ball" (97).

Although Stein distances herself through abstraction, she also personalizes her situation by frequent use of first-person pronouns. When the lover asks if she is accepted ("Can you be proud of me?"), she answers for them both: "We are full of pride" (107). By speaking for the lover, the narrator gains security and practices dominance. There is also reassurance in this inevitable dialogue. It serves to comfort her in her more daring assaults on morality.

The narrator's claims to irresponsibility in "Possessive Case" come partially from the fact that a homosexual couple's sex is not procreative. Since they do not create more life by their acts, they do not "have to satisfy a larger precaution" (120). They have to take care neither with their physical relationship nor with providing a suitable atmosphere for offspring. This freedom is only part of Stein's intricate and elaborate system of self-justification. She recreates herself as the hero of a narcissistic fairy tale when she speaks of being able "to marry for love and to be handsome and very clever and to be deterred by no difficulties and to give her attention to dogs suffering with wounded soldiers" (121). Her persona is alternately "shameless" and "polite" (133), civilized and yet boisterous. In answer to some bothersome voice daring the narrator to find someone superior to her choice, she can answer with the familiar disclaimer that she does not care for appearances and does not care if this indifference distresses anyone (142). A vague, generalized voice speaks philosophies of the flesh—"Is flesh advisable?" (147)—abstracting and distancing the argument until it is comfortable, taking the neutral position even after she has already chosen sides.

One of the more interesting "moral" tones Stein achieves is the coy *faux-naif*, one in which "there are some things a girl can't do" (150) and "I am delighted with that. You know you mustn't" (158). She metamorphoses from the practitioner to the reformer and back again. Philosophically, in "Possessive Case" and other works, she is of the "maximize pleasure and minimize pain" school ("We all want to be happy. I suppose and we do what we think will make us so" [151]), and she sometimes attempts to circumvent the problem of guilt, refusing to think of the past and resolving to live in the present enjoyment of the senses. This simple hedonism, however, does not prevent the narrator from scolding and quarreling with her own self-acceptance.

In Stein's extreme resolve to deal with the body in its full sexuality, she purposefully intersperses private references with a frank and flagrant style. Its erotic content is usually celebratory, though typically interrupted by parody. In Stein's use of different tones—whether she

babbles the baby talk of romantic love or has recourse to the shockingly
clinical—she always has in mind the diversity of possible ways to look
at homosexual love and at her love object. In this respect her writings
take on a cubist dimension, examining their subject from all perspectives simultaneously. Thus love and its fulfillment become objects, to
be shaped and molded at different levels of seriousness. But Stein seats
herself in her audience only to clamber back onstage without warning.
In her interior theater, the tension between how she is seen and how
she sees, of how she is thought of and how she thinks, provides the
sustaining energy for her eroticism.[3]

The author's intensely private voice—"I am so repressed and I can
state it, I can say. It was bitter" ("Pink Melon Joy," 354)—when it does
appear, only underlines the essentially theatrical, dramatic, "presented" self, the role of narrator, that Stein, by virtue of her narration,
cannot avoid. Predictably emphasizing the inevitable, Stein often interrupts her comments with the phrase "I said."

Often the narrator brings up the urgency of the act. It is a question
of instant relief or gratification ("Relieve me oh relieve me" ["Not a
Hole" BTV, 223]) and also of a wish, a shared desire, a culmination.
Her rhythms, much more than her logic, create a sense of inexorabil-
ity, necessity: "He wished it. She wished it. Ball" ("No," 55). The
flatness of the tone here provides wry humor, while her repetition
creates another kind of parody, with listing used as a mock-heroic
device. Her "enthusiastic" gushing catalogs provide gentler, touching
jokes. Little cries of "baby" and "sweet" ("A Sonatina Followed by
Another," 15) echo strangely in the face of the chivalric lists, in which a
courtier describes every detail of his lady's virtues in the most approving terms imaginable.

Some contexts are farther from the act of love than others, but the
difficulty comes in knowing, as both writer and participant, how to
make words correspond with sensation. In one typical passage she
throws many "linked words" together, each having a different emotional resonance, so that the final impression is a culmination of many
parts, each giving meaning to the whole: "Call it a lamb call it an
unpronounceable residence call it peacefully, call it with stretches call it
with withered . . . butter joy . . . obey it in leisure and earn and earn
nevertheless gentleman" ("Possessive Case," 135). One interpretation
of this passage might have the "lamb" referring to the innocence of their
relationship, an innocence Stein also exploits elsewhere with her use of
baby talk and her parodic romanticism. As their house is "not men-

tioned anywhere," it is also "unpronounceable"; "residence" has attached to it frequent and varied associations with the idea of the sexual organ. Other references in this passage deal with the couple's age, emotions, and attitudes about sex. Butter, like cake and water, appears frequently as part of Stein's special food imagery for sex. Sexual and creative urges come together in "leisure"—both are productive and should earn her (the gentleman who labors for his love) respect.

While Stein does offer a careful "presentation of self" in her erotic difficult texts, she also departs from public images dealing with identity, certainty, and roles to entertain more private images. Though humor is a primary technique, instead of presenting only the exterior surfaces of the relationship she insists on an "inside" look. She wants to reveal not only how Alice herself appeared and their mutual fantasies of each other, but also her private speculations on these fantasies. If the author usually maintains a hearty, joking attitude about her fatness, she can as easily show ambivalence toward it in describing the love relationship. She wonders if Alice sees her as exaggeratedly large—looking "fatter than ever" ("Painted Lace," 2)—and even while blithely declaring "I am not worried about breadth" ("A Sonatina Followed by Another," 20), she regrets "I should have been thin" ("Pink Melon Joy," 349). She can even become confused about what she does look like: "Do I look fat and thin" ("Lifting Belly," 110). Yet she can reassure herself that there are distinct advantages to solid, affirmed weight. She can be more cheerfully sensual because she is heavy: "all belly belly well" (65). The large body is architecturally imposing, creating a grandness, an expectation of "an arena to be monumental" (78), both a sculpture and a monument. She continually changes the "I" from tall to short. But while Stein herself changes from tall to small at will, Alice, viewed from without, is always small, petite, slim, whether as a child or girl or lady or man. The smallness of the beloved can be appealing but can also be equally unpleasant. Toklas's fragility makes her prone to be "anaemic" ("Pink Melon Joy," 351) and tense.

Stein's frequent punning games accentuate her meaning.[4] She combines religious and sexual prohibition to get "fairy ham" ("Lifting Belly," 106) and nationality with personality and shape to produce "levelheaded fattuski" (86). She demands and describes in the terse "Mount Fatty" (97). She shows her concern with procreation in her joining of "wide spaces" with "fertile soil" ("Possessive Case," 112). She also gives a sense of continental mass in her "expand my chest endlessly" ("Lifting Belly," 99). This ability to evoke mysterious relations between words both intrigues and delights with its vision of intensely personal experience. Her diction may be bawdy, yet it is assured, not prompted by an insidious or sly intent. Her tone is rarely that of a person telling forbidden stories, but instead offers a frank and playful treatment.

Stein's reliance on metaphor increases as she approaches more intimate subjects. She draws on literary tradition, particularly medieval and Elizabethan, for some expressions—such as "toy," "treasure" ("No," 44), "jewel" ("Pink Melon Joy," 350), "accoutrement" (356). These terms fit loosely with her "chivalric love" imagery—when she speaks of fair ladies, drawing them fairer, and so on—and also match the pseudo-romantic tone in which everything seems thrilling, wonderful, rich, and miraculous.

Stein also borrows from Toklas's sphere of influence, the domestic, for her private metaphors for the body. The domestic was as near to Gertrude Stein as the literary, and she always surrounded herself with the movements of an orderly household, so both cooking and sewing offered particularly available sources for sexual imagery (and indeed always have been part of sexual lore in folk and popular literature). Toklas's role of cook and seamstress enters into the scenes of lovemaking as she lights fires ("Possessive Case," 134), uses "fire irons" ("No," 38), doing "what was threaded" ("Pink Melon Joy," 349), "sewing it, really sewing it" ("Possessive Case," 140). Part of the richness of love comes from the sweets—jelly and cake that Toklas makes—especially when juxtaposed with sexual passion.

Eating and the fusion of oral and genital imagery provide the clearest introduction to her intermingling of all natural functions. As with romantic "baby" references, the world is evoked by her parody and shrewd humor, evident in "mouth and muscle" and "thanks I chew" ("Pink Melon Joy," 352), "satisfied with meat" and "cut me a slice" ("Lifting Belly," 86), "wedding jelly" ("A Sonatina Followed by Another," 17), and "did she say jelly . . . my jelly" ("Lifting Belly," 83). The body merges the domestic with the natural, moving inside and outside the home at will, first in the whole body metaphors (of mountains, Mount Fatty, for instance), but also in the specific metaphors of "climbing" and "blowing." The nature words mingle well with the domestic ones and remind the reader of Stein's daily life: that she had a luxurious garden, that she loved to walk for miles daily, that she had a sustained interest in sun and sky.

Stein uses the word *cow* with great effectiveness. If, as Richard

Bridgman suggests, it is involved in both the nurturing aspect of Toklas and some sort of birth,[5] it is also the orgasm, even the potential for it, as in this extraordinary evocation: "Pussy . . . full of a cow factory . . . manufacture cows by vows . . . cows are necessary after feeding . . . cows multiplied. By proper treatment . . . honeymoons . . . cows come out" ("A Sonatina Followed by Another," 24). While expressing the idea of sexual pleasure in this privately pastoral mode, she never attempts to suppress her "barnyard" meanings. She also varies her meaning of the word *cow* itself, so that it alternately bears the feeling of sexuality, the organ itself, food, protection, or the mythical idea of lesbian birth. (Occasionally Stein includes an ambiguous phrase on the theme of the lesbian couple having a baby—see "Lifting Belly," 90, and "Possessive Case," 119). It is both a derogatory female symbol (in the beast's placidity, stupidity) and a positive symbol of mothering and unselfishness, of pure animal sensuality and nurture in an Edenic world of simplicity and warmth.

Linked to these specifically natural images are those religious metaphors, especially of purification and enlightenment, that Stein uses to describe the sexual organs: "a cleaning thing" ("No," 37), "retracting glory" ("Pink Melon Joy," 349), "excellently seized" ("Pink Melon Joy," 358), "miracle" ("Lifting Belly," 72). The religious metaphors carry all the surprise of revelation and bring the natural metaphors of rain and wind to their ultimate expression in the idea of purity and cleanliness. With this comes the sense of being set aside and apart. Thunder, as orgasm, heralds the cleansing of the passions.

"Lifting Belly" and "Possessive Case" share some of the same vocabulary on the subject of masturbation and orgasm. From their titles on, they partake of a "secret" meaning—the "lifting" suggests sexual arousal, "possession" suggests orgasm, and the "belly" or "case" the organ itself. Both works develop the idea of sex as exercise, either sport or play, Stein's sphere, or domestic work, Toklas's sphere. In "Lifting Belly," the usages of lifting—"such exercise" (72), "good for me" (75), "bounding" (77), "I backhand for thee" (91), "recreation" (76), and "mixing" (73), all very healthy but "fatiguing" (76)—reinforce this idea.

"Lifting Belly" partakes of the purely joyful, sport, and play aspect of exercise (the organ as muscle), while "Possessive Case" portrays the flexing of sexual powers by using house metaphors that relate sex to the preparation of food, domestic organization, and movement about the house. Domestic words used here deal predominantly with cooking, especially baking, which Toklas enjoyed: "pressed" and "push"

(152), "raising and rolling" (156). "Mixing" comes from the kitchen
(113), while "it can be opened very easily" refers simultaneously to the
arousing of sexual passion and the removal of a tin top. This penchant
for opening also appears in "the care of opening the door" (120) and
"worried a window" (115), going and coming through windows and
doors ("A Sonatina Followed by Another," 26, 28) and "widening . . .
makes a door" ("Pink Melon Joy," 371). While Stein often associates
"doors" with body parts, her metaphor typically multiplies as well as
screens its meaning; "door" suggests alternate referents—an orifice,
the welcoming door of the Stein salon, or an entry to meaning within
the text itself.

Stein also borrows from male-oriented metaphors like "pulling" ("A
Sonatina Followed by Another," 23) and "drilling" ("Pink Melon Joy,"
347). She uses the vocabulary of inanimate objects such as fragile
glassware, to which something is done, to describe the feeling of cli-
max in "wonderfully shattered" ("Pink Melon Joy," 350). Fats, oils,
butter, water, are all featured prominently in both "Lifting Belly" and
"Possessive Case," where they can represent the bodily fluids.

Other action verbs in "Possessive Case," concerning sports, cleaning, or kitchen tasks, or even grooming, are among Stein's most
onomatopoetic and imaginative. If the vagina—an object that is "prone
to be propelled" (130), rather like the cars of which Gertrude Stein was
so fond—can also be thought of as a "box," intercourse becomes "they
box a box" (114). It is possible that "you just put me out each time. It's
enough. One two" (154) refers either to her boxing metaphor or introduces a new one, of baseball. A phrase like "visit gently" combines the
social with the sexual in a more quiet but equally effective way. The
active "male" world that reflects Stein's interest in cars and sports is set
against the "female" world of Toklas's more placid activities. Metaphors that mock the dressing table, like "I curl little Fanny" (118)—at
once "Fanny" can be thought of as a part of the body, a woman getting
her hair curled, and a stage name for Alice Toklas—also underline
Stein's dominance and control. In "Lifting Belly" sexual hunger
equates the organ with food, particularly "butter" and "meat" (86). In
embrace "we cut strangely" (67) and she whets the "knife" (83). Pastry
at its best, sex is "useful . . . warm yet light" (95).

A last category of metaphor incorporates the others but is not linked
to a single specific referent. These take Stein away from idiom and
parody and even further into private language, demonstrating how complex, varied, and imaginative Stein's associations can be. The reader

senses that these sections, while not susceptible to precise definition, are still meaningful. Colors join with feelings, shapes enter without being named directly, artificial verbs take the place of real ones in startling and controlled juxtapositions. Meaning is produced not by an act of the intellect but by a liberation of emotional associations. These fascinating "near meanings" circumvent and yet enlarge accepted language.

"Pink Melon Joy" reveals its mood in the violence of its metaphors, which very nearly produce linguistic orgasm. Stein, using words like "violences" (348), "chopping" (351), "established belt or tooth" (355), "I shook a darling" (356), "targets" (362), "commotion" (366), "reverberation" (368), creates an effective meditation on sex and mastery in marriage, the two becoming one by force, "aggregate" but "alone" (347), that allows the writer "excellent arrangements . . . suddenly . . . I rushed in. I was wise" (347).

The immediate world and its topographical features often provide a jumping-off place for these extended or generalized metaphors in "Lifting Belly." In her usual manner, Stein introduces the metaphorical environment in the first few phrases of her work. This is the case in "No," in which "I had a pretty good room" evokes an intimate bedroom setting with "fire, chairs and silver" (35). Inside the house, "honey" is accepted and "butter" felt. The house is cleaned thousands of times (37). The sensuality of the piece is set by the sumptuous furnishings of the "room": "black silk satin" (40), "quilt satin" (55). Somewhere a lion prowls, and one sees opened "fans" (55 and 57). Limbs are "rubber," they are "petted" and "carpeted" (63). Though occasionally these statements verge on the vulgar or the mock heroic, nevertheless the lover remains handsome, the house beautiful, the beloved romantic with her flowers, curls, and glances.

The generalized sexual metaphor in "Possessive Case" takes the reader to the heart of what must be, together with "Lifting Belly," one of the frankest of all Gertrude Stein's works. Her subject here is the seat of passion, described in every possible way and with ingenious imagination. Stein blends argot, domestic language, and hidden language, using open and velied words, replaying words she has used before in other contexts to extend and deepen the effect of her text. She introduces several long "runs" of prose that act as revealing "stages" or "scenes" of sexual release. In one such scene, "she" is "behind the window" and is then seen "leaping out widely" (136). Her surrender is sweet, the organ a "kind of cup" from which the lover is nourished. The act of accepting nurture is the total acceptance of the beloved. A last passage affirms the act in metaphors that have already been discussed: "Leaving a chair . . . liking a particular standing fire and not kneeling and using heels . . . with windows stream into bed, vital cake, vital candy" (155). Not only does method get discussed here, but body, house, and food are joined and harmonized.

Since Stein is never far from humor in any of her pieces, her frankest are no exception. The joyfulness and humor of her treatment of sexual themes break down social and linguistic barriers. The shock of juxtaposition of her unusual style forces Stein, as an observer and participant, into new and unexpected perspectives. Pushed by her own temperament to solve certain technical problems of rhyme and diction, to make up new words, to join others together, to treat her lines as a virtuoso singer might, Stein charms by the sweetness of her melodies, her sophisticated naturalness, her complex simplicity, her careful cheerfulness, her precarious self-acceptance. These private writings constitute her interior theater: she is the hero of an appreciative audience and the villain when the boos begin; and she is finally the audience itself, alternately caught up in the hisses and applause.

3

Characteristic Deformations in the Language of the Plays

Especially in the collections of her plays, *Geography and Plays* (1922), *Operas and Plays* (1932), and *Last Operas And Plays* (1949), Stein's texts are studded with "inappropriate" intrusions that appear to operate in areas beyond the author's volition. Disordered trains of thought[1] reveal inner equivocations and unresolved conflicts as well as those unexpected revelations that appear to surprise the author herself. These characteristic deformations are in fact characteristic defenses. But defense against whom or what? The nature of Stein's anticipated audience seems unsettled. At times she plainly fears they will disapprove or even punish her for her thoughts. At other times she treats them as confidants and even co-conspirators. Usually, she seems to imagine a series of idiosyncratic auditors,[2] close and distant, approving and disapproving, understanding and misunderstanding her.

Stein imagines both friends and enemies in her audience and alternately takes the part of each faction to dramatize her dilemma. "Can you be rowdier" ("Saints and Singing" OP, 74) she asks herself. Later in the play she replies: "Yes I mean exactly that. I mean to be very exact. I mean to call you, I mean to come, I mean to be especially seen and very nearly established. I mean to cloud the rain and to articulate . . . very clearly . . . and to pronounce myself as aroused. Are you aroused by him or for them" (81).

Stein's audiences, however varied, always contain one who would

59

question her purposes. Is she a lover or an exhibitionist? Is concealment needed to add piquancy? If Stein's words do not directly address
her concerns, her indirections do help emphasize her position, her role
as mediator between her attempt to "mean exactly" and her awareness
of her potentially dangerous audience.

This shifting writer-reader nexus is at the carefully formulated center of Stein's difficult style. Her evasive narrative strategies demand a
language that can be used simultaneously to placate and to startle, to
both say and unsay. The casual, disengaged, or unsympathetic reader
is to be amused and misled, the sympathetic reader whispered to and
courted, and the two relationships maintained simultaneously. The
effect of her efforts is both to compel and dispel her audience's attention. The stylistic contortions and characteristic deformities in the
language of Stein's plays can be read for their strategies of concealment
and revelation.

Although Stein's writing often assumes a bantering tone, it speaks
movingly of the anguish of being misunderstood, of needing a reader
who will participate vigorously in the act of creating meaning. Caught
in a web of words and struggling to be understood, Stein must use the
very obfuscating language that created her previous difficulties. In a
passage from "A Sweet Tail," she admits her need for a reader to
"rescue" her meaning: "Suppose a tremble, a ham, a little mouth told to
wheeze more and a religion a reign . . . that makes a load register and
passes best . . . gracious oh my cold under fur, under no rescued reading" (GP, 67). This monologue is in the conditional—"What if I were
like that and no one understood?" Of course, Stein is like that. Her
sexual and creative "tremble" is both emphasized and belittled by her
use of "ham," a word she frequently associates both with the idea of
meat in its folkloric sense and with Jewish dietary restrictions. The
"little mouth," a reference to the vagina, is simultaneously the writer's
mouth, "hamming it up." Her text, told to "wheeze," is made purposefully difficult. Her lesbian love, "a religion a reign," is identifiable both
by its serious and its "royal" nature. The whole "load" of her sexuality
must be interpreted by the reader, who either understands her garbled
message by correcting it and passing it on, or who misunderstands and
lets its truths "pass" unrecognized. This educational metaphor is explicit throughout Stein's difficult texts. Stein fears being unmasked, but
she also fears going unrecognized. If she is not read sympathetically, she
will become "cold," and her texts will remain safely nonsensical.

The reader's task is rendered still more difficult by Stein's constant
vacillations. Typically, she makes statements on either side of a logical

equation and seesaws back and forth between them, emphasizing both their complementary and contradictory aspects. Also typically, she will avoid direct mention of her subject: "If the message is sent and received and if the tunes have words then certainly there will be soon the centerpiece which has not been removed" ("Scenes. Actions and Disposition" GP, 113). Subjects must be approached with the greatest indirection. Only after examining the entire work will the observant reader find that the "tune" had "words" after all.

In the following passage, Stein can be seen carefully manipulating and overlaying her argument with sections of suggestive and distracting effects:

> Come in cubicle stern old wet places. Come in by the long excuse of more in place of . . . to cut a whole condition . . . all that can see the pen of pigs wide. All this man is a make of chins which is to be tall and most many women, in the directory that shows why the state which is absolutely with . . . plastering received with boast. All this in bedding. ("Old and Old" OP, 229–30)

Although the sexual nature of this passage is evident, its exact referents remain obscure. The language is twisted and reshaped, predictable syntax evaded and turned back in on itself. The "pen of pigs wide" is not only the sty of sexual shame but the author's pen that will ignore all expected decorum. Despite all, it will be "received with boast" by the sympathetic reader.

Codes not only keep some out, they also allow others entry. In "A List" (OP, 94) Stein says she must "change songs for safety": "Change songs for safety . . . if they were . . . differently decided . . . delighted . . . accidentally relieved and repeatedly received and reservedly deceived." The opposite dynamic is also at work, however; such language invites an act of recognition, an act of sympathetic interpretation. Even as Stein recognizes the danger of her position, in her trope of contradiction, her positive note is immediately clear. She claims to be "delighted" and "relieved" by both her writing and her life, indulging herself "repeatedly." Thus difficult and obscure, seemingly accidental, statements serve in fact as part of her intent and act as keys to both her reception and her reserve.

Intrusions and Denials

Stein's coding strategy is a willed and intentional process, a carefully donned mask through which she artfully expresses her thoughts and feelings. Her intrusion "errors,"[3] uncensored areas of her discourse that seem to intrude on prosaic statements and make them ambiguous, although very frequent in certain texts, are accessible through a similar analysis. These intrusions seem to enter haphazardly into her texts, creating a randomized surface. It is as if parts of the message have actually appeared against her will or as if Stein has no control over its development and logical direction.

Stein's basic technique for tolerating these intrusions is repeated complete denial. Stein seems almost smug as she describes an assumed historical identity, a figure called Byron, in the play of the same name, who "cannot be punished for the sins of commission and omission because partly and happily he earns nothing for any one" (LO&P, 365). "Happily he earns nothing," no punishment, and has thus effectively armored himself against the dangers and responsibilities of communication. For if Stein is ashamed of her message, then she must also be ashamed of her "system" of living ("An Exercise in Analysis" LO&P, 125). Stein's personae, with all their verbal armor, are continually exposed and ever vulnerable: "I should not have mentioned it" ("Mexico" GP, 328). So Stein is forced into thinking of different possibilities for "telling"—avoiding timidity but admitting remorse, affirming the "telling" by separating it from its content. The anxiety about "telling" can be quelled by not hearing what is being said.

She will insist that she writes "a work of pure imagination in which no reminiscences intrude" ("Paiseu" LO&P, 155). But in speaking of the imagination, Stein can make fine distinctions. What is "pure imagination"? "Come up out of there is very well said when the instinct which has lead to the introduction of words and music not pictures and music, not pictures and words not pictures and music and words . . . not words when the instinct which has lead to the spread of rubbing has been shed then we will invite each one to sign himself Yours sincerely Herman G. Read and very quickly I include everything in that new name" ("Objects Lie on a Table" OP, 107).

In the opening of this remarkable passage, Stein answers the reader who would have her "come up out of there"—out of her fears and prudishness, to reveal her secrets. The functional intrusion enters after the word "instinct," which, when repeated, seems to unleash the erotic mention of "spread," "rubbing," and "shed." By breaking through the barrier of "words . . . not words," the erotic language of the libido momentarily leads Stein to name herself "Herman" (her-man), referring to her marriage with Alice B. Toklas, in which Stein played the male role. The translation of this phrase can thus be achieved by a reordering of its elements. "Herman G. Read" becomes "read G (Gertrude), her man." Everything is included in that "new" name. But since the instinct referred to by "the spread of rubbing" (sexuality) will never be shed, Stein will never sign herself "sincerely" in this way. Clearly, Stein sometimes manages to have her imagination work both ways, purely and impurely, at once.

Stein's intrusions usually occur when she is trying to rationalize the problem of sexuality. Just as she is telling us that she will not reveal herself or that it is probably better not to be associated with the idea of sexuality at all, Stein provocatively emphasizes the sexual content of her associations. In the following selection, for instance, the intrusions occur as physical descriptions of the earth, drawn from the vocabulary of mining: "It is as well to be without in their reverberation in the meantime ways which are in opening to their site do unexpectedly deliver it as in a tunnel and they attend the opening and the exit" ("Madame Recamier" OP, 376). If, in the beginning, Stein seems to be begging the question of sexuality (using "reverberation" to refer to the movement of orgasm), the very mention of this word causes the appearance of associated kinds of sexualized geological images such as the earthquake or the explosion that mining requires, in turn producing other metaphorically related words: "opening," "site," "deliver," "tunnel," "exit." These words intrude on her originally framed denial to become a kind of contradictory approval of her original premise.

In the following example, flat denials again provoke a series of intrusions, as if Stein purposefully used an indirect method to prod her unconscious mind:

> There is no way of speaking English. What do you mean. I mean that anybody can begin and go on. And finish. It's easy enough and especially hard when there is a use. Why do you say exchange. I do not know what they say exchange. They say they believe in exchange. I often talk about nothing.

> What have I to say.

> I wish to speak to you what shall we do about water. The water is everywhere. Imagine me in bed. We were very careful to ask about it.

> Not for teeth. ("He Said It" GP, 270)

The intrusions function to change the subject, coming up because for her "there is no way of speaking English," no way of telling the truth

clearly, in a straightforward way. She will have to go "round about"—
allowing the thought to catch her unaware, mid-sentence, and inter-
rupt her.

These intrusions are sometimes present in the form of questions,
which must be answered truthfully as if they came from a real audience and she, as a writer, had a duty to address them. When repetition[4]
plays a role in these intrusions, it propels her into greater frankness.
Intrusions in Stein's work can also appear as a series of free associations, with the original impetus coming from some neutral key word.
Even seemingly noncommittal words like *it* and *thought* create these
possibilities: "It was mostly thought out by records and moist houses,
it was mostly thought out by moist houses that bedrooms should be
heated" ("Saints and Singing" OP, 73). Here again, even the concept of
writing about "it" (the idea of sexuality) makes possible "moist houses"
(the genitalia), "bedrooms," and "heat." These linked intrusions occur
because she has meditated on the impermanence of records; this challenges her to have something to record. What is most important to the
unconscious will eventually find expression, but the author's reluctance remains.

Words may be produced inoffensively but still have the most telling
effects as Stein alternately admits and fights off their implications: "I
do not wish to be married. I wish to be sure of marriage. I have
selected my sisters. They do embroidery. I will not copy them. I am
not so old . . . I do not pay attention. We do not pay attention to one
another. I am in a way disappointed. I do believe in fish" ("Do Let Us
Go Away" GP, 223–34). What is striking in this passage, besides the
inherently dramatic technique of interacting with an imagined audience, is her various considerations of the idea of marriage. Because
marriage is such an important word, connoting the idea of her lesbian
marriage with Alice B. Toklas as well as the conventional kinds of
marriages she saw in the society around her, she couches her first
mention of it in negative terms. Her very next sentence, "I wish to be
sure of marriage," however, has positive connotations—being able to
avoid loneliness and having a partner she has "selected." She modifies
marriage with her first intrusion, "sisters," as she modifies "sisters"
with a feminine activity, one she associates with Toklas, "embroidery."
Copying can be interpreted two ways: the author rejects the typical
heterosexual mold and also distinguishes between the type of woman
Toklas is and the type of woman she, Stein, represents. This distinc-
tion of roles leads into an assertion of youthful vigor, but that revela-

tion in turn triggers a disclaimer: I do not pay attention to what I write, and so you should not notice it either. The negative aspects of her sexuality and its positive elements, as in the fertility of a fish, remain precariously balanced. The fish imagery is remarkable in the sense that none of the preceding images prepares for it; it seems to well up from another more repressed source.

The more the speaker ornaments or disguises her communication, the more its strongest connotations will prevail: "I do see what makes me thunder when the words are not repressed" ("Reread Another" OP, 127). Her word strings can therefore be used to create meaning, however ambiguous, even if the words themselves remain anomalous—without clear or predictable relation to one another. Stein's words, as she observed, are "remarkable . . . in their resistance" ("Paiseu" LO&P, 165).

Typically the denial itself contains the essential "forbidden" material, but again surrounded by negative modifiers, as in "I am not a christian and I have no wife. Do be hot to-day" ("Reread Another" OP, 123). If we take the speaker to be the author, the first statement is true, the second is not, and the third discounts the second disclaimer. Such denials arise from anxiety over punishment and the fear of discovery: "What I am afraid of is that they will just attract an awful bombardment on themselves in which they will have to be supported. Oh no they won't do that" ("A Poem About Waldberg" GP, 166). The querulous side is comforted by the confident self, assuring her that no calamity awaits the speaker. The military metaphor, drawn from Stein's experience of World War I, suggests the destructive power she attributes to society and social norms. They are as capable of destroying the fortifications of her ego as bombs are of destroying a city.

Self-Editing

Stein's structure of denial suggests that it is not only the reader but the writer herself who both wants and does not want to know what she reveals. In her self-editing, she denies her real subject, avoids possible disapproval, and even cuts off discussion. In "Byron a Play," she speaks of excuses she has made for the lover, the ambiguous "him," and at the same time gives us a compendium of loving actions, the very ones her censor would have her hide. She stops speaking in this train of thought only after she has defined the steps in intimacy, inspired by her original attempt to shield the "him," her persona of lover. Stein continues to unfold her inner drama, carrying the speaker along despite the excuses that form an ostensible barrier between reader and author.

Though constrained by her internal necessities of self-censorship, she never shows confidence that her denials will be believed and accepted. In "Lynn and the College de France" (OP, 269), she wishes to hide an event (one day) and "declares" her "reserve" and "denial." But those words are goads to more ambiguous statements, like "Infuse. Joining. To petition," even as she promises politeness will come from such "joinings." Even when she succeeds in preventing her messages from escaping, their very presence in her mind can waken her fears. She wants to deny "there is [an] example in this," tells herself to be "cautious" and "restrained" (GP, 294; even the title, "Not Slightly: A Play," has negative connotations). In her role as editor-censor, denial itself forces her into admission. Every denial contains its antipode. The following passage is notable for its pairing of opposites, its divided structure:

> I please you as a dilatory victory . . . rub it . . . clean it . . . what are your passages. How often have you crossed the ocean . . . how very many are you willing to moisten rapid repetition with angular vibration. You are not angular, you do not vibrate nor do you caution men and women as to war and liberation . . . do divide beside . . . can you ring beside the use and air of elaboration and a vision. ("Saints and Singing" OP, 84–85)

This might be considered the "naive" mode of self-editing, the truth revealed and then quickly taken back, the extreme clarity of the many sexual words ("rub," "moisten," "rapid," "angular," "vibration") and her playful use of water ("ocean") to imply sex prompting a vigorous response from her internal censor, who exactingly replaces her positives and questions with negatives.

She continually warns us that her censor is awake and challenging her: "they are very careful. Of. Their memory . . . and their permission" ("Lynn and the College de France" OP, 256). "This must not be put in a book. Why not. Because it mustn't. Yes Sir" ("Bonne Annee" GP, 302). The very existence of her words in print is threatening. She does not want to oblige the reader with easy admissions of guilt. She admits "it is never to be safe to see that" ("Paiseu" LO&P, 158). She herself cannot be "seen" or interpreted by hostile witnesses or by any one who would remember what she wrote and implicate her, "if writing is in little pieces" ("France" GP, 27).

She wants to suggest "restraint and alarm and reserve and a mistake" ("Old and Old" OP, 224), hoping the result will be "no witness signing" ("Scenes. Actions and Disposition" OP, 109). Or she will mock her attempts at truthfulness through the use of rhyming mode, as in "it is useless to discover what they do in liking one another" ("Madame Recamier" OP, 365). She recognizes that the reader may understand her subterfuge, but is determined to continue her self-imposed constraints: "pleasure . . . so agreeable so selected and so fairly denied" ("They Weighed Weighed-Layed" OP, 238).

Self-editing takes many forms: it can balance, block, or modify a statement; it can take the form of a disclaimer that reveals the truth or an admission that temporarily removes her social mask. Sometimes her editor has to be satisfied with bringing out a disclaimer secondarily, too late to hide what has been said but better than no disclaimer at all. The editing may be naive enough to make us suspect that it also serves Stein with a tool in her pursuit of total frankness; her difficult passages force the reader to search all the more diligently and deliberately for their partially revealed truths.

Anxiety over Punishment

Stein's anxiety over punishment is an important impetus for her denial and self-editing. This anxiety is most directly involved in the act of telling itself. The more dangerous her communication, the more difficult its pronunciation. To shift the burden of guilt involved in the act of "telling," the speaker may imagine the communication to be coming from another, reducing danger to gossip and rumor: "I hear you when you say that you are a wife that you have been worried and that you have placed a cream where it belongs. A cream. And not a quarrel" ("Saints and Singing" OP, 76). The speaker gives credit to the "you" for admitting the marriage relation, but also acknowledges the other's "worry" (and, implicitly, apologizes for causing it).

Extreme care is useful in avoiding punishment, though the knowledge of this necessity brings recognition that she is not exercising sufficient care, or else she would not be thinking about being careful in the first place. "Say I am careful. Believe in punishments" ("Mexico" GP, 305). If the punishments were not so real, the subterfuge would not be so complicated. If she were not afraid, she would not ask whether "denial [is] . . . better than allow" ("Paiseu" LO&P, 158).

In one long passage from "England," her voices go into great detail about the symptoms of her anxiety over punishment, so much so that they resemble a physical illness. In the process of detailing the reasons for hiding her intentions, the persona reveals the range of public reaction that might result from her being "seen," as well as some of the activities that might expose her. This passage is typical in its resonance, its honesty, its prudery, and the sexual topics it manages to present with the attitudes of satisfaction and of self-condemnation both intact:

> A trembling that has an appetite, a refusal that has a nervous extremity, an expression that has a direction of disregarding . . . they show it and they caution it, they do not outrage giving it credit. The time does not come to anyone who is pardoned, it comes and then when there is patience when there is use, when there is talking and a table, when there is even a slice of ham, it comes then to be announced that certainly understanding is what is not partial, it is so kind and strong and lengthy that certainly there is no disgrace. (GP, 92)

The persona knows why she is trembling and why she feels nervous but means to "disregard" these symptoms. On the subject of the "it," so often evoked as a hidden sexual referent for Stein, her character will both "show" and "caution," giving "credit" or honor without outraging the audience. The listener is dangerous and must be placated. The concept of "pardon" gives the confession moral dimension and reminds the speaker of the need for "patience" because of her peculiar "uses." Nevertheless she admits that there is no such thing as "partial" understanding; she can only hope for kindness and strength and delay so that she does not disgrace herself in public.

Even when Stein focuses on the forbidden nature of her content rather than the attitudes surrounding it, she expresses a deep sense of her anxieties:

> That you see me
> Which you do do
> This makes a crisis in the life of Sweet William.
>   ("Listen to Me" LO&P, 411)

The knowledge that the persona has already been discovered ("which you do") will only push her language closer to the brink of the indecipherable: "Anybody shows something when something is showing . . . there always is some way to be reconciled to a difference" ("England" GP, 95). The persona moves between her own mores and those of the reader and tries to establish the "difference" while implying that it does not make any difference. The balanced tone is created by her unruffled understanding of how she must appear (what is done cannot help being known) and her attempt to continue with a conciliatory attitude: "She may be resolute if she was found nor will they cover this . . . they may be known as a wedding." This is yet another strategy to avoid punishment. If she does not seem guilty, perhaps no one will realize that anything is wrong.

Often, as in "A Circular Play," the character seems to be speaking about the nature of forbidden material. She addresses several idiosyncratic auditors in a kind of declamatory litany. Although she feels remorse after such forbidden conversations, she insists on "calling hearers." Not all the members of Stein's manifold cast of characters want to be careful, but all are fearful:

Fear can be in three places
Fear of yes
Fear of not yet
Fear of felt it as fear.
And so he came here
Not of his own volition
But once here
Accustomed to being here
With much enjoyment
To himself as well
This does not make Byron cautious with restraint.
("Byron a Play" LO&P, 367)

Some fear sexual gratification ("fear of yes"). Some fear postponing gratification ("fear of not yet"). Some fear without knowing why ("fear of felt it as fear"). By denying her intent but not her pleasure, Stein hopes to establish her identity without taking responsibility for it. Nonetheless her caution and restraint necessitate disguise, in this case a "historic" mask.

Excess of Subjects

The language of Stein's difficult texts is crowded with an excess of subjects. She allows the sensual world to flood her consciousness (like the New York School of poets—Koch, O'Hara, Padgett, and Ashbery) until its stimuli, fed in simultaneously, achieve an illusory and disorienting equality of significance. Katherine Anne Porter, for instance, complains in "Gertrude Stein: A Self-Portrait" (1947) that "wise or silly or nothing at all, down everything goes on the page with an air of everything being equal, unimportant in itself" (521–22). Van Vechten described something of this sort while discussing Stein's mosaic style of free recall: "She followed Cezanne's procedure of filling in every inch of space on the canvas with details, each of which is of equal importance" (LO&P, ix).[5]

Stein extends her associations so far that many appear to have "un-foreseen" similarities: "I can remember when the change occurred, I can remember . . . relieving . . . relieving . . . and really asking bless-ings . . . raised eyelashes, eyebrows and columns" ("Saints and Sing-ing" OP, 81). The humor and difficulty of this crowded statement derive from its surprising juxtapositions. The "change" could refer to Stein's change of gender, which is "relieving" to her and makes her ask others' "blessings" on her state. But the raised eyelashes of love will more likely give way to the "raised eyebrows" of the world than to the raised monumental columns she desires. The increasingly disjointed associations of this passage both mask and imply her sexuality.

In "Not Slightly: A Play," she admits that free association provides an oblique kind of display: "It was said and well said . . . and avoiding, it was avoided by instantaneous crowning it was mounted by sullen points it was suddenly anticipated and nearly by a trinket. What is a trinket" (GP, 299). Meaning can be suddenly revealed by the instantaneous crowning or mounting movement before it is explicitly stated or even anticipated. Here "trinket," like the words *jewel* and *treasure*, which Stein often employs, becomes part of her repertoire of sexual code words, which she often discloses and emphasizes through questions. Because of her inclusive style, the separate words do not necessarily connect; they come from different areas of association: "A list lost re-minds her of a fire lost. Smoke is not black nor if you turn your back is a fire burned if you are near woods which abundantly supply wood" ("A List" OP, 90). In this passage she circles around her central motif of "fire" in a free-associational manner, moving from its manifestation, smoke, to its fuel, wood. Even in this free-associational "run," however, the fire takes on an exceptional meaning for her, of sexual energy. She speaks of a lost list (of meanings?), which reminds her of her energy, its possible blackness or evil; and so, as she often does, she asks whether she really partakes in such activities—does fire burn near what abundantly supplies it? Does passion burn between lovers?

Word Salads

The free-recall method of Stein's composition, because of its tendency to be unselective and to overinclude stimuli, creates a word salad[6] whose connections are fleeting and unstable. Yet, as can often happen even with such obscure word salads as the one below, a general, if always deniable, meaning or intent develops as the passage continues:

> All pages and white thistles and little torn berries and little mass means, and the time of the stretch and a plan to carry poles and little searches and a couple of condies with a sudden best stick, and last met with a sign of a place to show touches and a little climb and a sweet hold of a more excellent and reseen oleander, a most excellent hurling, a most sandpaper and a glass which shows a change in cultivating rare trees and little things which are mutton and a pet all the same close bent share of cut a way clothes brush. The season is best with wheels. ("Old and Old" OP, 228)

Her images are drawn from writing, nature, food, physical objects, the body, animals, and even the mechanical world. Although the passage cannot be directly glossed ("condies" remains particularly mysterious), it unmistakably concerns areas of potential danger, which she expresses in terms of the natural forces, the thistles that can tear at her subterfuge. Her movements "stretch" and "search" and take on sensual overtones. Many other images intervene before she finishes with the chaotic but telling list of "cut . . . brush . . . wheels," terms that finally become a sexual joke and a pun on her love of driving: "the season is best with wheels."

The reader is caught in a long randomized word series with many connectives that hold the important words in a structure but are themselves not central to the passage's meaning. The important words are the covertly erotic ones that the other words only herald or connect: pages, thistles, berries, mass, stretch, search, stick, place, touch, climb, hold, sandpaper—culminating in the more overt "pet all the same," "close bent share of cut," and "a way clothes brush." Seemingly more explicit passages still retain the same sense of spontaneous, randomized expression: "A taste and a branch and a sucking of the day and the calm and the man and the noise so wettingly . . . there is no hidden treasure" ("Scenes. Actions and Disposition" GP, 114). Her nature imagery mingles with body imagery, which in nonchronological order describes the stages leading to orgasm. Through its imagery the passage also conveys the different areas of introspection Stein simultaneously creates, forming a mosaic of sexual experience; yet the disparate images do not lose their separateness and merge. They can be presented as stages or be allowed to recede into gibberish; the imagery partakes of both realities at once.

Word Showers

When the breakdown in Stein's syntax is complete, it produces noncategorizable word lists, a shower of words that bear only a sketchy affinity to one another: "Clinch, melody, hurry, spoon, special, dumb, cake, forrester. Fine, cane, carpet, incline, spread, gate, light, labor" ("III . . . Incline" GP, 189). Stein begins by creating a sentimental tone with words that connote romance: "melody," "hurry," and "spoon." Many of these words clearly contain a multiple referent. "Clinch," for example, and food words such as "cake" are often associated by Stein with sexuality. These sexual references also include "incline" and "spread," the "light" of orgasm, and the "labor" of procreation. But this freely associative structure could also be fitted to other meanings—for example, the domestic catalog of which Stein is so fond.

If the word showers can convey feeling, the strings of words that just miss fitting together can also be used to praise her love:

> They make it have what they like
> When they leave very much to them
> In their respect
> That they will have plenty of it
> As much as they call color
> In variety of making it have pleasure
> In their arrangement
> Which is violently
> Raised as a place
> In place of plainly for them
> In reality it is a measure
> Of their contentment. ("Madame Recamier" OP, 381)

Though the general subject is freedom, whole sections seem to be missing from the flow of the argument, as if another voice we cannot hear were answering her. The discreet "color" hints at emotion that becomes first social ("their arrangement"), then spatial ("raised as a place") and normative ("measure of their contentment"). She approaches the relationship with extreme delicacy; the allusive fragmented style does much to cover the argument and make the statement "merely" lyrical.

Rhyme, Rhythm, and Verbal Arabesques

Stein's verbal constructions often rely on rhythm and rhyme and verbal arabesques. These patterns of melodic sequences are often triggered by the semantic features of words organized through sound as well as through sense. Any reader can find Stein at work generating rhymes containing psychoanalytic significance: "In the way of rhyming. I can think of so much. Dirt, flirt and spurt" ("Land of Nations" GP, 408). In "dirt" she encapsulates her sexual shame, in "flirt" she introduces the acts and means of romantic love, and in "spurt" she humorously acknowledges both female and male orgasm. As in her "all like winking all like thinking all like sinking" rhyme, however, the dramaturgy of love is made more acceptable by its verbal context.

The same techniques are often extended in Stein's more self-consciously lyrical evocations. The saccharine tone of the passage below constitutes Stein's romantic mask for sexual feeling, containing her familiar baby talk. Even so, the obviously childlike rhythms mask her feelings and distract the reader from her content:

And then what do I say to thee
Let me kiss thee willingly.
Not a mountain not a goat not a door.
Not a whisper not a curl not a gore
In me meeney miney mo.
You are my love and I tell you so.
In the daylight
And the night
Baby winks and holds me tight.
In the morning and the day and evening and alway.
I hold my baby as I say.
Completely.
And what is an accent of my wife.
And accent and the present life.
Oh sweet oh my oh sweet oh my
I love you love you and I try
I try not to be nasty and hasty and good
I am my little baby's daily food. ("Accents in Alsace" GP, 409–10)

She gives us not so much meaning as a field of significance. She wills her love, denying her usual geographical, animal, and domestic imagery ("Mountain" as Mt. or mount, "goat" in its folkloric connotation of wild sexuality, and "door" as an escape or as a body reference). She is shouting, not whispering, about a woman who is more than just a "curl" and about physical acts that are more than just a "gore" or a brutal phallic attack. Her use of "winks" and "accent" implies an inner circle who can catch subtleties of tone and intonation. She will be neither quick to anger nor nastily hasty in the amorous "daily good" she does her lover. But the infantile appearance of the passage emphatically belies and belittles its content; by being a baby, she avoids adult sanctions.

Her humor is often her characters' saving grace. She can ornament her text with assonance and word-play as a positive approach to her forbidden subject. She can make her treatment seem innocuous enough with rhyming and syntactic manipulation to disguise or lighten her anxiety "with wishes and crosses and shawls and alls alls bells balls cover how do you do deniably . . . playful with a take be mine monkey shine lay low have a shadow of realise wise" ("A Bouquet. Their Wills" OP, 212).

The erotic context that employs childlike diction and rapid rhyming mode (both of which the reader associates with forbidden subjects) often appears when Stein uses the word *cow* to mean orgasm. But the self-deprecating tone of the following passage is at least as significant as the code itself:

> There was a good big cow come out.
> Out of a little baby which is called stout.
> Stout with kisses.
> There will be a good cow come out.
> Out of a little baby I don't doubt.
> Neither does she covered with kisses.
> She is misses.
> That's it. ("The King or Something" GP, 125)

The innocent tone here has a mocking edge; she is too coy to be taken seriously. The content is made to seem anything but passionate. Parody and euphemism transform meaning.

If Stein's verbal effects are dazzling, and often dizzying, that is exactly their intent. Content and authorial responsibility for meaning are undermined, as in the following example, where each word seems to be taking off from the last, in a seemingly inevitable chain, of "guide and. Divide . . . and preside . . . to abide . . . Bestow. Ours. Are all mine," or "everyone applies. Love and cries. And tender ties . . . to relate . . . the care. They take" ("Lynn and the College de France" OP, 285, 287). Nevertheless, the speaker is the "guide" of the reader; the "divide" can refer both to the body and to the acts that divide her from others—acts over which she "presides" as the dominant figure, about which she is loyal, "abiding," and on which she bestows all she has in emotional terms. Everyone "applies for" enjoyment, "love and cries," has "tender ties," even the author of "self-generating" texts.

Rhyme similarly submerges problems of meaning; because words sound alike, we accept their interrelationship. Verbal arabesques, moving quickly from phrase to phrase, overcome argument. The reader who manages to leap over such difficulties is assumed to be a co-conspirator: "It is not only known as a cow but now . . . address . . . press . . . caress . . . express . . . stress . . . kindle and confess . . . waving it alight" ("A Lyrical Opera Made By Two" OP, 58).

Progression and Suppression

Stein's techniques are remarkable not only in their stylistic excesses but especially in their power to suppress the reader's attention to meaning. At their most theatrical, Stein's techniques draw attention so completely to the surface of the text that the reader will not notice the gap between Stein's real subject and what she allows herself to say. But it is precisely this synapse that must merit our critical attention.

Words appear to come before Stein as equals, each as significant as the others. No overtly rational order constrains word production. Her inspirations appear to come from many directions at once. In the following selection, for instance, Stein uses many references to love, generated from her typical natural and domestic metaphorical bases of "roads," "irrigate," "rub," and "roll." Each is given the same emphasis; there is no progression, only accumulation: "Call all coupling just that please and a way to irrigate is a fountain . . . a heated moan . . . all so soon . . . sudden and a pole . . . miss old age . . . rub roads, roll extras . . . no pleasure pillows. . . . And bowels and butter and points and points" ("Old and Old" OP, 22). Here Stein's content clashes with her presentation. She says she wants to be direct and to avoid euphemism—"call all coupling just that please"—but the resulting text is just the opposite of straightforward discourse. She moves from initial statement into a rhyming and rhythmic section where her references are all synonymous. She remarks on the suddenness of pleasure, laughs at herself, provides alternate physical expressions but ends significantly in an equivocal denial, "no pleasure pillows." This denial, this expression of contradictory feelings, often in a humorous context, typifies her difficult style:

> A miss and bliss.
> We came together.
> Then suddenly there was an army.
> In my room.
> We asked them to go away
> We asked them very kindly to stay. ("A Circular Play" LO&P,
>   139)

Everything here is mirrors—reflections lacking the thing itself. Her punning on "miss," rhyming with "bliss," the contact, the "shadow phrase" ("arm in my womb") reflect emotions and sensations she both wishes away and welcomes.

But suppression itself can become its own progression, as in Madame Recamier's speech below, in which she switches swiftly from argument to argument without punctuation: "Most it is in inclined that they like it for them instantly made surely in exact in shuttling it without theirs and they have found that it is named at once like theirs in that ready to be eased in any place which makes understanding settled in theirs . . . it is caused as an incense to our fires" ("Madame Recamier" OP, 377). This passage has that strange off-center quality Stein often achieves when she omits direct referents. Later in the same play, with the image of "open" thought, she puns with a similar sense of vague sexual references:

> In between time.
> All of it shown
> With them
> With there and here
> A joint and open thought of whether it is well to varied in and on
>   account of measure and a choice of treasure. (380)

She is "in between," part of a thought that must be purposefully left "open," justified by her "measured" but unidentified choice. The text is fashioned as both an apology and an assault.

As much as Stein enjoys her role of educator, at such moments she is unwilling to admit openly that she can "say anything." What communications she does offer have a driven quality, as if the whole message had to be brought out quickly, even without punctuation. In some of her most compressed statements, she follows an intricate internal program whose symbolic elements are set within a hallucinatory context:

> I hear a sore.
> Stop being thundering.
> I meant wondering.
> He meant blundering. ("A Ciruclar Play" LO&P, 140)

Even in such extreme passages, the text remains readable, though open to various interpretations. The "sore" she hears instead of feels may be the "sore subject" of sexuality, but through a comparison with the Freudian "wound," it also suggests female vulnerability. One voice commands an end to "thundering," which is associated with wrong-headed "blundering" and the creative, open-ended "wondering," which here recalls "wandering," another familiar word in her repertoire. (Stein uses "wandering" as a euphemism for sexual experience in "Melanctha.") Wandering has traditionally strong metaphoric associations, as in the work of Dante and Spenser.

Open-Private Structuring

Open-private structuring of discourse,[7] in which truths are revealed intermittently, means that Stein's persona can be surprised at what it has uttered: "He can accidentally witness what he can mean" ("Saints and Singing" OP, 78). "The tone of surprise is uplifting but there is not that disgrace . . . is it astonishing. It is" ("England" GP, 88). Often, the connection between open and private structures is reflected in Stein's use of ambiguous pronouns. In "Places resemble their mother" ("An Exercise in Analysis" LO&P, 120) and in "A common place which is their in with it" ("A Play of Pounds" LO&P, 247), the third-person pronoun, having no clear referent, begins the private discourse.

She uses the vague "they" to indicate forbidden subjects: "They will be remarkable they will coincide they will account for it . . . they will

be in distress they will have it as an advantage . . . they will like it
clouded . . . they will put back what has been put away" ("Madame
Recamier" OP, 385). Again her statement equivocates, allowing the
relationship to exist in society (they are the same, they "coincide"
naturally, and they will "account for" why they are together). Her
repetition and use of a negative modifier (we "will" "put away" infantile pleasures—we will not enjoy) are balanced by the idea of "putting
back" what has been "put away" through repression.

The public "they" assures the persona that she is morally safe no
matter what she chooses to say: "By which they relish all at one time a
little at a time not when they make it for which no one adds more than
is careless to remind him has he done it. A manoir is in use" ("A
Manoir" LO&P, 288). Besides utilizing the punning meaning of
"manoir" (the residence, home, center of sensual pleasure) that could as
well be read "man-or" (woman), the persona appears sincere in her
appreciation but couches it in characteristically negative terms.

The "I," although often surrounded and camouflaged by other pronouns, can also speak, of course, but in a different and more vulnerable
way, ultimately more metaphorical and abstract:

> Biting meant mining.
> Shall he find it out.
> There is much to say.
> An opportunity in sizes.
> Further.
> I can scratch.
> Not it.
> Spool.
> She meant it again.
>
> . . . .
> Frightened.
> There really is no reason to believe that.
> ("Not Slightly: A Play" GP, 292–93)

Her many questions concern readers as well—Shall they find it out?—
while the statements and the voice egging the writer on "further" come
from a more approving alter ego, which asserts "I can scratch" and "she
meant it again." What should be private has become public, and the
public voice is suddenly frightened, placating, assuring us that what is
heard may not have been meant, but with an ungrammatically equivo-

cal "their" instead of "there." Thus the open-private alternation of discourse helps Stein transfer meanings from one area of consciousness to another, though she would prefer to confuse the reader and even herself about which mode she is operating in at any single moment: "You are certainly aroused by the apple the descent from the cross and the dog and the squirrel. You do please when you please" ("Objects Lie on a Table" OP, 106).

Connectives are virtually useless, or worse, unless they link congruent ideas. When Stein writes, "Really any authority is in the language and singing is not a victim" ("Scenes. Actions and Disposition" GP, 117–18), the "and" confuses more than it clarifies. On the one hand, she asserts the power of language, while on the other, she modifies language to "singing" and denies that it can be mistreated by the listener. The two sections seem random but are actually diametrically opposed. One argues from a position of strength, the other from weakness; but both speak to the same point, the defense of the writer from a hostile audience.

The open-private structuring of Stein's plays, characterized by her shifting and ambiguous referents, is the key to their continual leaps of associations. When her public narration begins to read like a heavily edited film with too many missing frames projected at too rapid a speed, her private narration is likely to be most eloquent: "Many have the same in came and all the light is many wet all the burst in in the man and best to hide is only sweet. All is that and a little haste, a little pleading . . . all is chance to be the curl that sets and all the winding causes" ("In the Grass" GP, 75). Defense (many people act the same way) leads directly to sexuality and orgasm ("in came and all the light is many wet"). Feelings "burst" in the "man" (herself) whose act is somehow forbidden and shameful ("best to hide"). Her contradictory closure, "is only sweet," simultaneously affirms and denigrates the experience. "Haste" and "pleading" are chronologically switched. Selection, association, and referent are all equally alienated from their normal function. Instead, especially connotative words, like "wet" and "winding," become basic to her narrative. "All the winding causes" are the accidental and uncontrollable processes that Stein uses to release the potential of her language, so often at odds with what she thinks suitable to express.

Ambiguous neutral referents give Stein the power of "arranging substance," "reciting her pleasure" ("They Weighed Weighed-Layed" OP, 248), without making it too easy for the possibly censorious reader to condemn her. She evades her disapproving interest as well as her own feelings of guilt and with this technique elaborates and refashions material for her approving audience, in the process becoming intertwined in her increasingly dense language. She moves further from her associative stimulus and her specific referents, using words as starting gates to her own interior life.

Multiple Errors

The ungrammatical nature of Stein's language may be the single most alienating feature of her experimental style. Even her excessive repetition, punning, and continual sexual jokes do not discourage readers as much as her disordered sentence structures, the important elements of which are often omitted, substituted for, or masked. This denial of standard syntax strikes some readers as a form of infantilism, in which normal speech exists only as a kind of mockery and self-disgust. She creates many different kinds of "errors"—phonetic, semantic, phonemic, syntactic, pragmatic, both grammatical but meaningless, and ungrammatical, with or without meaning. These difficult passages often are interspersed with brief moments of greater clarity, and they seem to be randomly scattered throughout her plays. The "error" can be as subtle as a few changed letters:

> They engage them.
> In fortunate allowance.
> .   .   .   .   .   .
> Thank them in eddying.
> .   .   .   .   .   .
> It is falsely an alliance. ("Say It With Flowers" OP, 342)

Here, besides the fact that the whole thought rests in contradiction ("fortunate" versus "falsely"), she has "confused" two important words, "allowance" (what is given, what is allowed) and "alliance" (as in marriage, already hinted at in her word "engage").

Another kind of "error," this time more obviously a mistake, occurs in a passage such as "I could be widen as out loud" ("Lynn and the College de France" OP, 275). These few words suggest a familiar, considerably expanded statement, such as "it could be that I widen as much as I say it out loud," but one that still remains ambiguous.

Perhaps the most frustrating of the "errors" Stein makes is the "grammatical but meaningless" type, usually revolving around the question of diction. French linguists define this quality as *folie discordante verbale*, which could mean either gibberish or glossomania. Such sentences are structured as if intended to mean something, but their vocabulary seems inexplicably random: "The least license is in the eyes which make strange the less sighed hole which is nodded and leaves the bent tender" ("A Sweet Tail" GP, 67). The syntax is fairly clear in this passage, but the word choices are not. The sentence gains clarity because the verbs are in the right position: ＿＿ is in the eyes which make ＿＿ the ＿＿ which is ＿＿ and leaves ＿＿. However, the significant "wrong" words—license, strange, sighed, hole, nodded, bent and tender—do form a composite emotional and physical image of marriage. Of the two levels of this sentence, grammatical and meaningless, the "meaningless" part provides a vehicle for the unacceptable content, while the grammatical structure appears bland, empty of any particular meaning.

Stein is also noted for long passages composed of several different kinds of "errors." A message may be flawed simultaneously in the semantic, syntactic, and pragmatic areas. This fragment from "Civilization, A Play in Three Acts" suggests certain philosophical verities about the writer's life in a frank but playful way. Enough words from Stein's private or coded repertoire come up to help us gloss the whole despite the range of irregularity:

They may call girls girlish.
With or with or without
mention or nor no adding waiting.
Could they carry a that
they may.

. . . . . .

A father is faded not a mother.

. . . . . .

Civilization suggests enters.

. . . . . .

A moon. They need to have good weather.

. . . . . .

With which they will relish.
That he is more than leave it. As a pleasure.
It is a wife who has joined with a mother
and they need not be neat because or gather that they will add
   neither.

A father.
The grandfather having been dead.
. . . . . .
Or wood.
Or would she.
Be fond of leaving.
Open.
But not
after nightfall.
The entrance as a door. (OP, 50–51)

On the semantic level, she makes several words out of other words (girls, girlish, with, without) and uses punning, rhyme, and assonance (with, which, relish; wood, would). Redundancy (entrance, door) combines with syntactic awkwardness ("or nor no adding waiting," "carry a that"). On the level of pragmatic meaning, these difficulties obscure but do not obliterate Stein's message. If civilization is to be opposed to sensuality, the passage can be understood as a discussion of sexual choice. "He is more than" (he seems), she hints, but the censor replies, "leave it," abandon this subject. Mother and wife have joined and fused in the couple, while the male family figures are absent. Again, questioning breaks out: Would she be fond of leaving (the entrance, the door) open? Denial quickly follows: not at nightfall, the most predictable and vulnerable time.

A more complex statement, again involving the unmeshing of similar words, is "Pariah arrive . . . welded calls proclaiming . . . discover in a . . . pier" ("Paiseu" LO&P, 164). On an unconscious level the statement revolves around travel and makes the reader think of Stein's own autobiographical journey to Europe and her marriage with Toklas. The writer herself was a pariah before arriving and finding her "peer," her equal, her partner. "Pier" generates three ideas: travel, a "peer" or equal, and a partner in a "pair." Or the initial letter and last syllable may create a mirroring effect, as in the fearful "Should it be curious / Could they be cautious" ("Short Sentences" LO&P, 319). This embedded effect involves rhyming, assonance, and word-play, and it depends on the reader's assumption of the opposite of what is said: Why is she using the word *cautious* if she is not afraid of being incautious? The semantic relationship of the words often serves the same veiling effect:

Go in deer. Dear what. A saleing soon.
This was a boat.
In. Knows. Necessary.
No's necessary. ("A Bouquet. Their Wills" OP, 203)

Words transform as she questions her invitation with "dear what," but she moves into punning with "saleing . . . this was a boat." She follows with the repeated "in" to emphasize sexual ideas, as well as the play between "no" and "know" in the reconstructed statement "I know that in is (is not) necessary." The transformation of the word "no" moves from "know" (the necessary knowledge of her activities) to "noes" (a grammatical "error" and a partial statement that "no's" are necessary) to the clear, at least grammatically "correct" statement that follows: "No is necessary."

Cannibalization

In "III . . . Incline" Stein uses a different technique of dissembling language. Here she allows her words to "cannibalize" each other, sounding like parts of the other, either through alliteration or repetition by mirroring syllables and fragments of words, to comment on her own techniques: "Any counseling non consuming and split splendor. Forward and a rapidity and no resemblance no more utterly. Safe light, more safes no more safe for the separation" (GP, 180). She discusses the "split splendor" of her writing in language that is specifically sexual. But even as she mimes sexual motions, she denies the "resemblance" of her private language; it only causes a further separation between her life and the lives of others.

Another way Stein has of embedding and cannibalizing previously used words is by adding or changing a prefix or a suffix. This often creates words at cross-purposes.

And they will like
They will have it alike
In their dependence
And independence. ("Play I [III]" LO&P, 202)

She links differences with sameness, perhaps illustrating the irreconcilable opposites that go into a marriage and the struggle for freedom and autonomy in the posture of "dependence." A similar use of "like" is more bawdy but ends on a romantic note of assonance in "Where is it that they like they look alike. With this. Kiss" ("A Lyrical Opera Made by Two" OP, 56). Liking becomes part of being alike, the kiss part of "this" and also "this kiss," the special way the couple have of interacting.

In a different but related technique, the same word transforms itself in three different ways: "Justly divided . . . and dividing and defense of division" ("They Weighed Weighed-Layed" OP, 238). The couple can be thought of as separate beings as well as a unit. The word *divide* undergoes transformations: in one sense it is their separateness, but in another it is their openness (they are divided, they divide for one another) and even their united defense of their acts to the world. In an equally condensed embedded statement, Stein combines the familiar disclaimer with rhyming and repeated syllables: "Not begun which is why they mount in amount . . . they refuse wish for relish" ("Byron a Play" LO&P, 335). Although some act is "not begun," yet it is begun, for she goes on to describe the act that "mount[s] in amount." The mirror effect of the words contradicts yet affirms a circular statement in which potential ("wish") is actualized ("relish"). The semantic "error" of frequently noticing previously uttered words allows for multiple and sometimes contradictory and confusing meanings and also enables Stein to enjoy her usual word-play with some unusual results. The surprising and difficult passages that follow rely heavily on abstraction and metaphor to create an artificial landscape of the body: "All the wedding shows the spring to be the place where water springs . . . all the dwelling shows that escaping is not an escapade" ("England" GP, 92). The "spring" the wedding shows also contains a reference to the genitalia (the place where water springs), and that "dwelling" demonstrates that her rebellion, "escaping," is not mere adventure but is meant as a serious involvement.

Repetition

Stein's immersion in mirroring words leads her inevitably to repetition and gives her security within a restricted vocabulary allowing her to rely on the unit of the syllable rather than on the word. Stein tells us how important repetition is to the establishment of an authentic voice: "Repetition . . . stability . . . precaution . . . accentuation . . . and attraction" ("Capital Capitals" OP, 69). By disrupting syntax, repetition also forces the reader to be responsible for content: "If you can repeat it and somebody chose it, somebody shows it, somebody knows it. If you can repeat and somebody knows it" ("A List" OP, 103).

She often combines repetition with other difficult techniques, like nonsense runs, as in:

> Miss curls and hard chests and all best and little mutters. Little mutters to salt wet words, little mutters in the dew. Little is the case. Little is the case. Go belt, go in there copiously and within and strong sudden salt works . . . have cold wet nurses and cold wet noises and cold wet nuts . . . cup spaces are . . . local . . . always coincident . . . with long angels and much much passes, much so. A little gain is a squeal it is . . . the first apron it is the second. It is. Collusion. Collidable and covered." ("Old and Old" OP, 227)

This nonsense run repeats many key words as well as creating similar words and using a mode of rhyming. While the first sentence begins with a description of the beloved ("miss curls") and suggests both whispers and mothers in "little mutters," the idea that both lovers are "little mutters" stresses the emotional source of this love language. "Dew" could mean "do," and the repetition of "little case" could suggest sexual coding, as it does in her bawdy early work "Possessive Case" (1915). The writer encourages sexuality in "go in there copiously," calls the lover a "nurse," and describes the act in opposite language, "cold" instead of hot. She includes more erotic suggestion in "cup spaces," calling the hands of the lover "long angels," using the repeated "much" as a veiling word (many forbidden things happen, or "pass"). She explores the similarity of the lovers in a domestic metaphor ("the first apron . . . is the second") and evokes mystery in the faintly sinister "collusion" of the act of love, which both "collides" and is "covered." Repetition becomes a disguise that relies on multiplying words, letters, and syllables and that creates instant replicas for key words.

Examples of this technique, with slight variations, illustrate these frequent clockwork responses. She exhibits perfect confidence (on both sides of her sexual dilemma), as if the repetition itself gives it the label of nonsense and discourages us from reading any more deeply: "No monotony is necessary since I do visit. You do visit, yes I do wisely to visit where my visits are appreciated" ("A List" OP, 98). "Visiting" allows the persona the freedom to come and go, in a social and in an intimate context. Repeated visits are a way of talking about the couple and its joining, its communion: "They said he said . . . two centers . . . two surroundings . . . and they centre, and their center, they centre, they do not centre here" ("A List" OP, 102). Both the pronoun switch (to transfer guilt onto the "him") and the "twinning" are keys to meaning. The change in spelling of "center" indicates her perception of the slight difference between the couple, who are the same and yet are not, as they are also "sisters who are not sisters," as in Stein's piece of the same name. The metacommunication she practices depends on mutations of words and resonances of association. Repetition, which usually denotes stasis, becomes instead a technique to generate continual change.

Inner Life

One constant in Stein's work is the domination of themes from her inner life. As we have seen, the words used to describe this inner life often intermingle and shift their meaning within a single passage, reflecting both past and present visions of love and domesticity, her varied roles, her work, and events from her daily life. Part of her portrayal of an inner life is accomplished by selective playing of roles, especially of famous historical figures, usually male. Byron is one such figure, a favored romantic guise Stein uses to explain her artistic world. When she is not writing, that character ceases to exist: "As being dependent upon being seated / If the one seated rises Byron falls" ("Byron a Play" LO&P, 371).

She takes on Byron's name and, with it, his power. Both are centrally concerned with the act of writing. Whether the historical characters possess her or she them is constantly in question. Their union is indivisible at times: "Sometimes he compels her to carry him" (373). Because she can make the decision to "carry him" as a character, she can equivocate about the subject and even see it as a burden, something to be ashamed of:

> Lay Byron down
> Escaping Byron.
> Byron makes no attempt to escape. (383)

In the first statement, the censor gives an order, but in the second the role itself escapes, the inner reality dominated by a war among the character, his role, and the author's willingness to continue to assume that role. This may also be a way of saying inspiration is leaving—no, it is not—a dialogue about Byron's ability to be both persona and muse.

In the role of "writer," Stein concerns herself centrally with the relation between sexuality and writing and the need for honesty in both the treatment of that relationship and the discovery of her true subject: "No happy day and the best is there and there is everywhere. Say it all in the morning, put it off in the day, have it come in the evening, use the tune every day, say it and please the organ, laugh and remain the same . . . coming has a day to stay anyway some way that way. Full and the tune, a shaking of the ends . . . if there is no exercise . . . ("Scenes. Actions and Disposition" GP, 113). She writes about the difficulty of creation, the way it can change an unhappy day of the ineffable day the "there" was everywhere. The urge to write or to love can be "put off" at one time and taken on again at another, and that is the subject or tune she uses to "please the organ." She reiterates her satisfaction at her choice and ends with an abstract description of the intermingling of sensual and intellectual pleasure, "a shaking of the ends" of the pen that "exercises" by speaking out.

Material from the inner life may become obstreperous, with gross associations or unacceptable images intruding from the unconscious, with the censor suddenly unable to screen out primitive drives: "They prefer oysters with widening areas. / They leave out which is way amount" ("A Bouquet. Their Wills" OP, 199). Transposed, the last phrase would read "they leave out (that which) is way (too much)," with a pun on "a mount."

This kind of material rises to public view in fragments, vivid shapes and sensual assaults (in terms of sight, taste, and smell) that mingle and shift in space: "Collecting poles . . . a cost in corsets . . . a cold flower, a bad flavor, a certain decent and . . . a request for a distant smell" ("Old and Old" OP, 223). She makes plain the cost, the negative aspects of love—"cold" flower, "bad flavor," where "decent" implies "descent," and the nonetheless continual desire. As this passage goes on, it becomes more abandoned and frenzied, and certain characteristic words surface, intruding on her thought. Words group together and look familiar but change when examined closely: "A little bit of spoiled choice . . . we . . . wake cake . . . hold with a piece of half . . . hold in with a canter and a choice . . . we in between . . . so allowed wonder struck . . . we change what . . . in . . . we in between . . . a log a handle" (223). The section above speaks disapprovingly and approvingly of her choice, "spoiled" but "cake," still sweet, eagerly assented to ("a canter and a choice"); we who are "in between" are "struck" with "wonder" at the enjoyment the body can bring. Why should she change this "handling"?

Stein's intrusions and intermingling of the inner with the public life can cast doubt on the whole idea of a play and transport her content to several different areas. Her phrases may come together with different levels of discussion, as in "Photograph," in which her sensual obsessions also fit her original topic and provide a curious double reading as she uses the language of photography and the language of drama interrelatedly, allowing certain words to intrude and forcing the reader to make sense of them:

> Photographs are small.
> They reproduce well.
> I enlarge better.
> Don't say that practically.
> And so we resist.
>
> . . . . . .
> So that the house chosen has a soft wall.
>
> . . . . . .
> Oh come just for one minute
>
> . . . . . .
> Two a twin.—Step in.
>
> . . . . . .
> Twin houses.
>
> . . . . . .
> Two twins have two doors.
>
> . . . . . .
> They do come together but some come
> more frequently than others.
>
> . . . . . .
> I can sigh to play.
> I can sigh for a play.
> A play means more. (LO&P, 152–54)

If the whole passage is a kind of welcome, the open civilities, the social comings and goings of the Stein *ménage* form a dominant metaphor for private and intimate relations between the married couple, the hidden reality of domesticity. She fluctuates between the image of the private life seen in her mind's eye and the public reality around her every day. Her florid pronouncements on sexuality have their counterpart in the daily courtesy the married couple show to friends; she also explores what the couple, and especially the speaker, is like. The next insertion seems to be sexual, and the following puns on the social and sexual meaning of "come" (which she uses in much the same way as she does the word *visit*). The couple, with their two doors, are "twins" in sexual identity. Her last insertion puns on the double meaning of "play," the structure of what she has just said and also its content. She refers to the idea that she uses code ("I can [cipher] a play") and that a play does not exist solely on the page or on the stage but also in the mind of its creator.

Stein's obsessive concern with aspects of her inner life is especially evident in her frequent use of heavily image-laden words meant to transform their immediate context. The accumulated effect of any single passage is therefore greater than that of any single part. Below, "Banking" introduces a cataloging section, and banking is particularly appropriate, since it involves putting away things of value or having things of value hidden away and also reminds us of Stein's special use for the word *treasure*, for example. She can even pun on the word *change* to mean her own change and that of the bank: "curving, summons, sparkle, suffering the minisection, sanctioning the widening, less than the wireless, more certain. All the change" ("III . . . Incline" GP, 189). Some of the feelings that come from this passage are sensual (as in "curving" and in "suffering the minisection"); some part of the message is Stein's usual imperious approach to sexuality ("sparkle") and her approval of sexual acts ("sanctioning the widening," "more certain"). The inner life comes through each word in a concentrated way; the words do not fit one another but do glow with the intensity of the same interior transport.

Apart from their manifest inscrutability, the most notable aspect of these texts is their supersaturation in the fantasies, hopes, fears, vanities, loyalties, and hallucinations that dominate Stein's inner life. No association is too trivial or mundane for inclusion as part of Stein's psychological landscape. Aided by revelatory "slips of the tongue" at vulnerable rhythmic points in her texts, Stein crosses the boundaries of the ungrammatical, the inessential, and even the unspeakable. The reader becomes an explorer of the texts' phonetic and semantic wildernesses, while the writer is ever busy changing and revising the maps, reestimating location, and planning strategies of flight and defense. Stein's complex verbal geography is marked by circumlocution and association, including repetition and redundancy, abbreviations, ellipses, verbal arabesques, ambiguous words, and other uncategorizable forms of metacommunication.[8]

Conclusion

For the most part, Stein's difficult texts pursue simultaneously two contradictory goals—to conceal the author's deepest feelings by drawing excessive attention to the surface of her text and to extend her experimental narrative technique to include as much personal information as possible. In pursuit of these goals, the torrents of Stein's words and images form ragged whirlpools around the obsessive foci of her attention. This pattern is not merely a case of Stein's verbal and conceptual structures being loose or freely formed. Her melodic sequences and rhetorical patterns are presented in ways that seem to grow not out of a poetically sophisticated sense of the line or a logical argument, but from vivid internal visions and forces over which the author appears to have little or no control. Any stimulus or referent can serve her as a springboard for transformation. Her imagination leaps, inevitably and compulsively, through inner space. But because this is a double leap—employing a simultaneously open and private methodology—Stein's difficult texts, especially her dramatic texts, appear at first to be nearly inexplicable. Her thought sequences seem broken or random; the construction of her sentences appears crude, primitive, or repetitive; her logic becomes questionable; her errors and narrative strategies seem designed to serve the express purpose of disguise or evasion.

Role ambiguity,[9] her diverse and inappropriate role identities, emphasized by her use of drama as an expressive mode, gives way to tone ambiguity,[10] her delight in the inappropriate tone or mood, her omissions, her silences. Stein all but completely effaces standard syntax and semantics in alterations, deformations, and transformations, which appear to become a sort of glossomania, signalling the reader's attention to the surface of the text at the expense of all else. An overattention to purely musical and rhythmic suggestions—such as rhyme, alliteration, and rhythm—sacrifices semantics to phonetics, producing a *folie discordante verbale*, a language functioning as an object in itself, quite apart from its identity as an instrument of communication. Her manipulation forces knowledgeable readers into a special relationship, one of "rescuing" her meaning, based on their willingness to persevere in the face of verbal anomalies and accumulating "errors" meant to distract unsympathetic readers and evade Stein's own internal censors:

They may know. That. One is one.
In made. To punish them. With one.
It is. An anxious thing. To say . . .
With which. They will. Please. Me.
After all. It was not what. I had expected. It. Was you.
It was you. And. They. Will have pleasure.
In that case.

. . . .

They will be anxious. That they have. Seen me. ("They Must Be
   Wedded To Their Wife" OP, 173)

4

"Guardians and Witnesses"
Narrative Technique in
Useful Knowledge

In *Useful Knowledge* (1928), a collection of previously unpublished shorter pieces written between 1914 and 1926,[1] Gertrude Stein makes the case for "redress" and "excess" (200) in our sexual and imaginative lives. The composite text is a dramatic collage of changing styles, alternating between distinct voices and various roles. Its most inventive bursts of free rhythms invariably give way to tight rhyme schemes and exact meters. Surprising juxtaposition is its most basic resource; resonance and fluidity are its basic procedures. Of the twenty-one short works collected in *Useful Knowledge*, none provides a constant narrator.

Instead, as in *Geography and Plays*, Stein continues her earlier practice of role-playing, this time by evaluating her own relationship with Alice B. Toklas and attempting a first experimental autobiography, whose sequel, *The Autobiography of Alice B. Toklas*, would appear in 1933. In that book, she would use another entire personality as a mask. In *Useful Knowledge*, the language itself functions as both primary vehicle and disguise. It is as if her extreme need to speak the unspeakable forced its way into a new channel—a way to both say and unsay at once.

In *Useful Knowledge*, Stein takes special delight in submerging her questions and lists, with their extensive sexual puns, into a distanced scientific and philosophic language. As in a philosophic inquiry, the questions asked are often "leading questions," which sharply narrow and carefully determine their response. Yet in another sense they also provide Stein with a release and a way to go forward—a technique that cuts through the themes of the book and allows her to step in and manage her own, and her audience's, perception. By using leading questions and philosophic "proofs" to convince us her suppositions are correct, she balances between oppositions and creates extremes to dramatize all the sides of her argument. She addresses herself to a novice who needs instructions (hence the title), but she remains intensely conscious that her words will be overheard by a disapproving general audience, composed of guardians and witnesses, internal as well as external, bound to local values and traditional social behavior.

As often in such situations, Stein develops a sort of secret code that the novice might understand while the guardians may not.[2] "Would it seriously threaten anyone to be cowardly to offer to write and say something" (9), she asks. Here, as elsewhere, Stein's words bounce back and forth between crazy mirrors, interchanging positives and negatives. Therefore, "not to be cowardly" is as much what Stein means to say as "to be cowardly." And, of course, since she is being "cowardly" to use code at all, she can draw attention to her own fears.

This code is often arbitrary. She may put in one negative and take out another or reverse the statement and say the opposite of what she wants the reader to hear. Though this procedure is frustrating to some, it is an important technique for Stein herself—it shocks her out of her normal syntax and helps her to locate new forms while remaining at least partially hidden and protected. No wonder she continually reassesses the clarity of her symbolic language, which validates her claims to being a teacher—worrying "can you tell them this bliss?" (107), and asking "How can a language alter?" (108) as well as questioning the appropriateness for her purpose of the "disguise" of philosophic reasoning, "how can you reason about that?" (110). Of her Socratic questioning, she asks (with a pun on the hymen): "Can wisdom be curtained"? (108). She questions both the initiate and her presumably disapproving audience: "Is it necessary to change?" (20).

Her basic problem, stated through repetition, can be summed up in her questions "What is the difference and why do you marry?" (164) (what are the differences between homosexual love and heterosexual love, and what are the necessities of both?). The role-playing of man and wife generates much of Stein's metaphor and energizes her thematic preoccupations with dominance and submission and freedom of sexual expressiveness. When she speaks to the question of whether she has hidden anything she hopes to reveal, she "invents" a phrase that includes a pun on lovemaking, "do we secrete anything?" (14).

To help her say many things in many voices, all at once or almost at once, Stein creates different distinct metaphorical fields in which her work as a whole operates. One such important field of meaning is the general analogy between the nuclear family and the homosexual marriage; another is the analogy she creates between the body and geography. Stein has often associated "natural images" with sexuality, but in *Useful Knowledge* the pattern is especially clear. She begins coyly, telling us the book is about "romance" and "owning the earth just as pleasantly as ever." She plays on this analogy successfully throughout, but its sexual significance—"arousing the land" (166)—must be inferred by the novice. In terms of the audience at large, she remains at least partially disguised—hiding behind the sense of passion she links to the general idea of any ownership or possession. This possessing, as we will see, is usually by a member of the family group.

The "geography" of Stein's sexuality has to do with dominance, as in conquering territory. *Useful Knowledge*'s writer roams over the body, a previously unexplored map, and takes it over, disregarding danger, recording the new cartography with an almost exultant sense of duty: "Explorer . . . occupies successively the places . . . he recognizes . . . so that he will later be able to make maps of the region which he has traversed" (32). The section "Wherein the South differs from the North" extends this metaphor by associating Stein herself with the warmer, more emotional South and Alice B. Toklas with the colder, more intellectual North. But the piece is also a dialogue of id and superego, of the free-speaking sexual prophet and the censor, both resident in Stein's personality. When the two speakers finally unite ("North and South nestles," 29), Stein's conciliatory "there is no need for opposition" (23) can be understood as being only a partial truth. Duality is central to her procedure, as her purpose is to conquer the guilt in the regions of both the body and the mind: "It is in the interest of the North that this is told, it is in the interest of the South that this is told" (34). These maps are puzzles, mazes, dangerous journeys. Their very inaccessibility only emphasizes their fragile and vulnerable nature. Even so, the explorer might enjoy the difficulty of the terrain.

After the delights of discovery, Stein tells the novice the land must be claimed as an extension of the explorer's self, as family, that it must be owned as well as recorded. "Can you give me the regions?" (78) she asks, and "we commence to supplant" (164). This territory, once entered, must be made safe from the incursions of other lovers-artists-travellers. It must be claimed by the family group.

Like the imagery of geography, imagery of family relations provides Stein with an important and charged metaphoric field. Lacking a family she could accept, or one that could accept her, Stein creates all these roles herself. Mother, father, and sibling to her beloved, Stein is metamorphosed into all possible relationships, molding the family to suit her own requirements. Julia Kristeva's essay, "From One Identity to Another" (1980), traces this same metamorphosis in terms of the separation from dependency on the mother, "whose instinctual and maternal semiotic processes prepare the speaker for entrance into meaning" (136). The speaker achieves identity through "breaking away" from this original source, retrieved only as "displacement, condensation, metaphor and metonymy." Kristeva explains this link to the mother in terms of a "continuous relation" that is broken and repressed, only reappearing through the use of poetic language that can reactivate "this repressed, instinctual, maternal element" (136). She equates language with the establishment of incest prohibition, but calls poetic language, "for its questionable subject, the equivalent of incest." This helps explain how Stein's poetic language in *Useful Knowledge* is used to reestablish forbidden links.

Speaking to the novice, Stein uses the intimacy of familiar associations to play on the incestuous implications of lesbian love, as well as reflecting, in a distanced, humorous way, mostly for the benefit of the wider audience, on her own complex family history and the acceptability of her present conduct. Using the locale where she lived with relatives and went to graduate school (1897–1901) in "Business in Baltimore," Stein's persona marvels at the jumbled chaos of the family tree when a lesbian relationship both parallels and displaces the nurturing love of mother and of sibling: "Placed and placing should a daughter be a mother. Placed and placing should a mother be a sister altogether" (74). By untangling the new relationships with the meticulous detail of the anthropologist, she can use its metaphors to describe her own mode of loving: "Can you love another mother?" (111). By considering the homosexual couple in terms of a family, Stein finds metaphorical and explicit ways of displacing, describing, and admitting to guilt.

As with much of *Useful Knowledge*, fearful autobiographical material, specifically dealing with the early part of her stay in Paris (for example, moving Alice into her apartment in 1909, which led to Leo Stein's departure in 1913), resurfaces for further assimilation. Darker images point to her suspicion of family hostility and of the inevitable rejection implied in choosing the lover over the nuclear family: "In the shadow of our brother we have eaten" (104). Other "shadowy" references surround the choice not only of the ways that parents and siblings might disapprove but, even more, of the reaction of the outside world. But the wider her imagined audience, the more she feels called upon to reveal and then to defend and then to conceal her repudiation of conventional morality.

The following passage reflects the kind of complexity Stein continually builds into her encoding of homosexual love: "If we mean mother and daughter, black and black caught her, and she offers it to me. That is very very right and should out below and just so" (92). The reference to the family directs her into a private reference about guilt ("black and black caught her"). Her generalized "it" includes love, both physical and spiritual. Her affirmative phrase "very right" disguises the suggestion of orgasm, which, though not specifically mentioned, "should out below and just so." "It . . . should out below" both physically and figuratively, but mostly in her writing itself, which follows "below" in the text.

If both the natural imagery and the family imagery function to retell and to conceal her autobiography, these purposes are reinforced by Stein's innovative narrative techniques. By switching pronouns around and using rhyme and rhythm to deliberately give the feeling of nursery-rhyme nonsense language, Stein can reassure herself that the compressed biographical and erotic materials that she records will be subsumed under the strangeness of the stylistic presentation.

Thus, though Stein keeps pointing out the changing landscapes and recasting her biography in terms of geographic journeys, she is most concerned with moving Alice into her apartment with herself and her brother in 1909, though this is never directly mentioned. She prefers to dwell on her move from America to France six years earlier. Stein, simultaneously a political and a sexual exile, now seems to challenge the language itself, though she still retains fierce American and heterosexual loyalties. The paradox of Stein's situation is dual—although she loved America and was proud of it, attesting to that love in her autobiographies and histories (*The Autobiography of Alice B. Toklas, Everybody's Autobiography,* and *Wars I Have Seen*), Stein chose to live her life abroad. Similarly, although she was a lesbian, she acted the role of a man in a conventional marriage and gravitated to the men she invited to her salon, leaving Toklas to sit with the wives. Again, everything functions as a form of disguise—the wishes she wants to "bestow" are specifically sexual; everything is a combination of command and seduction: "Why don't you visit your brother with a girl he doesn't know and in the midst of emigration we have wishes to bestow we gather that the West is wet and fully ready to flow we gather that the East is wet and very ready to say so" (84). Her direct experience all but disappears, only to reappear in the guise of a private geography which, by its juxtaposition with the seemingly unrelated family material, points the reader toward the interpretation she intends.

In the following passage, her mention of *cows*, already an emblem for sexual experience, especially orgasm, in her work, provides just such a key. The "he" is, again, Stein herself: "He originally cultivated cows. After that he joined himself to all of them and after that he was as helpful as he could be . . . he had made what was to be attended to. That does make the difference" (133). "Cows," "joined," "nearer," "made," "attended to," and "make" are neutralized erotic references— "attending to" them makes all the difference.

In "Emily Chadbourne" (the name of a friend of Stein, but also "I'm a lie" . . . "had borne"), Stein is like land up for barter, but she is "not a saleable surface," not the romantic ideal for her times, and the choices for such women are few. "A surface that is too rigid is ruined, a surface that is loosed is smiling, a surface that is mine is mind" (88). The autobiographical information is hidden behind terse, all-encompassing metaphorical statements about the freedom, ownership, and cohesion of her body. Both physically and spiritually, her body is scattered throughout the book, awaiting a reader who is also a lover—because "a surface that is missed is widowed" (88).

As Stein's speaker is the surface of the land, enjoying the tilling of the beloved, she is also the text in the knowing hand of the reader and the elements of nature, enjoying the primal experience of love that the earth recounts with an "organic wit" (153). In extended musings about the effects of the "weathers" of love upon her, she alerts her readers and deepens their response as she moves deftly from one image to another. A typical meditation begins in rain, associating emotion and moisture, and ends by describing the feeling of orgasm, all in terms of nature and the natural elements: "I don't like rain. I don't mean that thunder scares me. You know very well what I mean. I mean that sometimes I wish I was a fish with a settled smiling center. I think it is an ugly word" (11). Stein interjects her direct statement ("you know very well what I mean"), the voice of her revelatory self, to help the reader—and herself, writing the passage—to recognize what her submerged subject is. Instead of feigning innocence about her admission, she chides the reader for not recognizing it sooner. Once she has achieved this focus, her private "natural" associations (the fishy smell of the vagina, the clitoris as "settled, smiling center") can be introduced. As usual, negative and positive are switched—the passage moves from denial of sexual desire to its full expression, though ending with a gesture in the direction of conventional morality. What word is ugly? It is, of course, the one she does not use.

Stein's major imagery is particularly vital because it often achieves synesthesia in its punning effects. Thus, "repeated leopards" (13) puns both on the sound of "leap on" and on the visual eroticism of the leaping cats, who were the beasts of Dionysus. When she counts "pansies" and lives in a "fruit house" (142, 157), even a list of states will become eroticized. "Kansas" will become "can's ass," while "Indiana" will become "In Diana," in the virgin, even though Stein is ostensibly remembering, as Mellow has observed (341), the home states of certain World War I doughboys.

The book's title lends resonance to Stein's methods. Her "how to" manual links her sexuality to her experimental writing. Both display the same reticence and versatility. As Stein tells us, "I learned to correct snatches" (12). The closer Stein is to sexual meaning, the more fanciful her technique, the more vivid her imaginative associations, the more developed her need for narrative disguise:

What a cake. What a kindness.
What a smell. What a shame.
What a slight. What a sound.
What a universal shudder. (12)

Only a reader who acknowledges Stein's actual sophistication can fully appreciate this text's mocking edge. The "cake" suggests both her sexuality and her text, whose unsympathetic apprehension will bring "shame" and "a universal shudder." It is for this reason that she immediately fuses the compromising material in this passage with the kind of automatic denial the reader has come to expect: "I will not be coerced. But I was. / I was coerced. I see it" (12).

Her abrupt truths and graphic descriptions are thus deflected by her tactful evasions and apologies. This mode, however, is not meant to interfere with the education of the novice, who must learn to "copy all the special ways of sitting" (8). Finally, the art of the text lies in the interaction between revelation and concealment—"the emphasis can be where you like" (12). Her attitudes toward sexuality are accessible if cryptic—each passage offers its own epigrammatic maze, which the reader negotiates at his or her own peril.

The nonsense argument, so difficult to refute or even to respond to in a coherent way, is useful to Stein as an effective means of disarming her audience. It is the centerpiece for much of the stylistic virtuosity throughout *Useful Knowledge*. Its mystery, its obsessive motifs of guilt and its autobiographical content, its sexual puns are all reduced to a childlike doggerel, the broken flow of "inappropriate" sections that disguise circular affirmations of her difficult "information." Her whole manner informs the reader that she does not mean to argue her points at all, merely to display and disguise the virtuosities of a stylized verbal dance. Without any direct reference to homosexuality, she can argue simultaneously for and against it: "It is a disease. Is there any way to stop it. There is a way and that way was the way that was shown to be their way. Dear things" (9).

Such circular argument is bound in contradiction. The basic insolubility becomes indissoluble—each half requires the other, even after the two halves are joined and the seams of the joint erased. In nonsense, Stein can use her dilemma against itself and explore the options of not resolving the antithesis in her formulations. In terms of Freud's theoretical constructs, Stein both "blocks" and "denies"—she represses the manifest meaning, and, when it appears, she rejects it, but in such an obvious way as to show she recognizes both her surface and her "deep" meanings. "In *The Interpretation of Dreams*, Freud showed that an idea's emphasis, interest, or intensity is liable to be detached from it and to pass on to other ideas, which were originally of little intensity but which are related to the first idea by a chain of associations" (Laplanche and Pontalis, 121).

The problem or contradiction that Stein brings up most often, stated simply, is that she isn't "supposed" to be married to another woman—which parallels, in terms of her own writing, her realization that she isn't "supposed" to use language as she does: "I don't think you can say that this is too natural" (11). But if nonsense is composed of sense plus a negation of that sense, then Stein controls her sexual and artistic rebellion, creates a pattern for her writing, from the traditional idea of sense merged in nonsense, the wise man in the company of

fools. If she begins by affirming her "fall from decency," she can then
deny her affirmation, going with the social standard in an argument
that is always circular and contradictory: "This is the way it has to
be . . . and not to do it again . . . she has absolutely promised never to
mention birds" (139). This is at once a neutral reference and a bawdy
reference; Stein expects the knowledgeable reader to remember folkloric uses while the naive reader just sees a non sequitur.

Of course, the negation can be most completely fused with its opposite when one is actually imbedded in the other. Then the very denial
becomes, like a kind of absence or a kind of silence, a reason to suspect
"hidden" meanings. The nonsense code requires denial of any intention, while nevertheless remaining involved in the content.

Stein's rhyming is a central vehicle for this technique, providing its
own dizzying and hypnotic circularity. The rhyming in *Useful Knowledge* pervades and lulls, giving Stein more energy for revelation, because rhyme, like denial, takes her ever forward, into the trance of
unexpected truth. Like an ecstatic shaman, Stein riffles through her
improvisational cards until they begin to make sense: "History is told,
will he be a great man will he learn to fan, can fanning be fun, can we
satisfy a nun, can we seize what is won, can a tall man hold a gun . . ."
(109). In this passage, history and the idea of the great man—
remembering that Stein liked to think of herself as Caesar—spring the
text into erotic fantasy. The question the passage poses is: Can a person
learn to satisfy himself outside the accepted norms? Stein "invents" the
image of "fanning" for masturbation, neutralizes the "I" with a "we,"
replaces the "lover" with a "nun," but includes her code word for
sexual mastery, "seize," which reminds her of "Caesar." "Caesar" reap-
pears at the end, in the form of a direct hint to the initiated, as a "tall
man" instead of as a "short woman," holding the offending organ, a
"gun" that goes off with the explosion of orgasm, which is simultaneously the pen of the writer, forcing truth into the text.

The rhythmic and rhyming sections of *Useful Knowledge* offer Stein
an effective mask. They also work emotively, submerging the reader in
her subtext, where the same idea can be stressed repeatedly, with short
variations, enforcing its intensity, convincing both reader and writer of
the inevitability of the actions described: "In heights and whites in
whites and lights, in lights in sizes, in sizes in sides and in wide, or as
wise or wiser. This is not to be the first to know" (66). Readers who
notice any transformation in this section, she writes in the last lines

above, should not expect Stein to explain herself. It is wiser and safer never to be the first to indicate knowledge of such matters. Knowing about "in sides," as she indicates by punning, makes them "wiser"— especially if they remain undetected so that no one will be the "wiser." The section above resembles the "in wed led" section of *Four Saints in Three Acts:* "in wed in dead in dead wed led in led wed dead in dead in led in wed in said in said led wed dead . . ." (*Selected Writings*, 609). It can mean something or not, depending on the reader's preference.

Nonsense and the nonsense rhyme protect Stein's content against disapproving censors, internal and external: "I like it descriptive. Not very descriptive" (UK, 79); "This is the use of a guardian, where it is guarded it is as well guarded as ever" (UK, 154). Paradoxically, as she meditates on the idea of constraint, constriction, and censorship, her own fears of being revealed provide a way to go on, a method of underlining those themes that she might otherwise suppress. In this process, she is very much like the young writer whose enthusiastic erasures only attract attention.

Stein's discussion of guilt always has a double edge. Underneath her denial, an affirmation pushes through. Underneath her affirmation another negation waits. When she cannot show all sides of her feelings directly, the suppressed point of view surfaces to torment and mock her. Where she speaks of traditional sex roles, her tone is childlike, but this reassuring style often parodies her message. Rhyme and nonsense provide Stein with a mysterious power to project her problems against a backdrop that seems nonexistent, impossible, laughable, and therefore not threatening:

> The scene of the future.
> Can you wish that jelly
> Can you wish that jelly
> Can you wish that jelly
> be eaten with cream. (105)

When Stein creates circularity with her rhymes, she also injects mystery that unravels itself, mystery always ready to offer an answer, even if that answer is just the reverse of the answer just given. "Nobody knows how open and how closed it is. Nobody knows. It could be taught" (136). The more she immerses her writing in this medium, the more she appears to resemble Lear's fool. Mystery gives a too-

blatant subject subtlety and humor, which somehow purge the eroticism of its profane quality, soften it, make it easier to accept, as if
laughter sanctified the act.

For this reason Stein often narrates autobiographical sections in
nonsense runs that sound like a mixture of half-formed stories and
baby talk:

> I come suddenly to be there and to be exciting. It
> was worse than money.
> Alright I will be natural.
> B is for birthday baby and blessed
> S is for sweeties sweeties and sweetie.
> Y is for you and U is for me and we are
> as happy as happy can be.
> . . . .
> Is reading painful? (12–13)

After her revelation in her first sentence, her second blends remorse
and desire. Sex, or "it," is "worse" or even greater in its effect on her,
than money, both of which involve "possession." By speaking of being
"natural," she gives a customary nod in the direction of respectability,
but by far the longest section contains the famous sentimental baby
rhyme to Alice B. Toklas. Mellon calls this "doggerel sentiment" (169)
but misunderstands its intention. The last question, "Is reading pain-
ful?" could be considered as a "follow-up" to the passage. By avoiding
the "pain" caused by the uninitiated reading something shocking, she
can avoid feeling this pain herself. Only a small portion of her audience, internal and external, "understands" the "useful knowledge" she
offers here. Because she uses only key words as touchstones to invoke
her whole information system, the reader must actively grapple with
the content and recreate it. In this way, she outmaneuvers the passive
audience of guardians and witnesses. To return to Kristeva: "The poetic function . . . makes of what is known as 'literature' something
other than knowledge: the very place where the social code is destroyed and renewed" (1980, 132).

Stein's persona, like an oracle, will come forth with a garbled proph-
ecy only at a certain kind of command. She often stops to remind the
novice, to compress and to catalogue, to reprise the knowledge she has
offered, though covertly, in her persona of teacher: "We know about
blame and circles and now we know about considerably added cur-

rents. The currents that come there. Where did you say. Call me louder" (165). A possible gloss of this passage might be that the blame attached to the "circles" of the female body creates "considerably added currents" in her lovemaking. "Call me louder" could refer both to the attraction of the forbidden, which calls her "louder" than accepted behavior, and also to the need for the reader to use greater understanding in "calling" Stein's meaning from the text.

Family reference, like geographical reference, can lead to both fantasy and resolution, especially when incorporated into Stein's difficult lyricism. In "An Instant Answer or a Hundred Prominent Men," for instance, alliteration releases a sensuality that compels Stein first to revelry and then to self-consciousness: "How often do we dream of daughters. Can you color it to satisfy the eye, can you. Can you feel this as an elaborate precaution. Can you. Who won Mrs. Kisses. Who won you" (145). As the irrational and the aesthetic converge in linguistic playfulness, they also remind her of the need for chameleon changes, protective coloring "to satisfy the eye" in the retelling of her own courtship—"can you feel this as an elaborate precaution"?

Of course, in this chaos or jumble of family members, in the exchange of one for the other, the nature and function of sexuality become diffuse. In terms of the family romance,[3] identity has fragmented—from the central core of the nuclear family, her identity has become diffuse. Stein continually reflects on role displacement and the complexities of sexual differentiation under her revolutionary system: "If to have and to turn over the edge and to have returned a mother to a father makes it as a mixture of later. Not late at all. To them both" (59). She deftly combines the two ideas, of "turning over" her sexual identity with "going over the edge" into the madness of switched identities and "returning," somehow, at least in terms of her own definition. She has been transformed, changed from a "mother" into a "father"—since Stein thinks of herself and Toklas as a couple in a conventional marriage—and this discovery of her true self comes not too late to give satisfaction "to them both." Stein's ability to transcend the expected limits is extended through the mysterious nature and function of her erotic and literary activity, a style in which "they" "reinstate the act of birth" (96).

The persona can step in and out of the roles of teacher, philosopher, scientist, family member, farmer, or explorer, as if they were a series of Chinese boxes. In each case, she rehearses her unequivocal duties as the subjects for her art, in order to lead the novice on while the speaker remains hidden from her internal and external guardians. Her very need for secrecy forces Stein into a new and strangely powerful language, its sexuality contained by an equally surprising prudence. Thinking of her "exercises," both sexual and literary, she says of herself: "He does not elaborate exercises. There are witnesses there" (146).

5

"An Autobiography in Two Instances"
Imagining the Reader,
Early and Late

███████████

The Open Context of "All Sunday"

In works spanning the first to the last decades of her career, Stein's self-censorship is accompanied by exhortations to readers to accept and understand her. As she says in *Wars I Have Seen* (1945), "Of course I was one" (24). In *Narration* (1935), she continually prompts her reader to recognize her subject, "Do you begin to see what I mean by this thing?" (22). She urges herself throughout to communicate, "Share it with them" (269), as she writes in *Mrs. Reynolds and Five Earlier Novelettes* (written from 1931 to 1942, and published in 1952). She is well aware of the nature of her texts, the language she uses, and the enacted, or prepared, quality of all speech: "We believe that most people when they make a noise make it with the intention of deceiving" ("All Sunday" AB, 107).

"All Sunday," a work written during her Majorcan exile in 1915, is a relatively open text. Like other pieces written at the same time, it celebrates intimacy and connection with the body. But the mixed identity of her audiences makes Stein expose her material in curiously framed utterances like this extended commentary (and rejection): "It is easy to be pleased. Regrettable. Circumstance. They make noises. They do this on the roof. Thus they avoid arrest and they continue to be gleeful" (105). Her fear of "arrest" is a constant, but so is her need to communicate. She can retain her essential identity even while rehearsing a more conventional response—"Regrettable. Circumstance."

Censorship and display combine to present a paradoxical double stance: "I do mean to offer paper and I do thoroughly reasonably chuck out what has hitherto hindered office of origin" (177). Here Stein offers herself as a new father—an "office of origin" might have implications for sexuality, creativity, or both. She says simultaneously: "Not this again. Knot this again" (187); the "knot" and the "not" are both evasive strategies—one she has created herself, one the repressive society provides for her. "I can always be proper. I remember what I see . . . I said it. Oh no don't come. I was very pleased. I cannot endure descriptions" (116). Or, as in "Short Poems": "Guard whole in a no necessity" (BTV, 45) or "Shield. Shield why" (128). In the first, the covert meanings are held in a punning context, in the second, in a psychoanalytic one.

In "All Sunday," as in many of the pieces in *Alphabets and Birthdays*, when the body enters the text, the commonplace contains the shocking: "I wish I could describe hands. I think your first idea was better. There is not enough continuation in hands. They're too different. It's too shocking" (89). Two lines later, in the section "Handsome Sunday," whose title puns on the idea of hands, she remarks, "Hands have been mentioned . . . I am surprised" (90). And yet a few lines later, in "In Pebico," they surface again in an affirmative mode: "I say let us have hands. I especially mean it" (90). Her last reference, in the same section, is to "pretty hands" (90). With the accumulation of repeated motifs, she validates her first idea but realizes that she cannot continue it—homosexuality is too different, treatment of lesbian sensuality is too upsetting, as would be the recounting of any part of her fantasy life. So she must feign surprise at the "discovery" of the repeated image—only then can she affirm its beauty and its eroticism.

Certain key words do not even need repetition to stimulate associations that disrupt the more guarded writing. In the following section, also from "All Sunday," a few such key words transform the stereotyped phrases culled from the language of the barnyard and the body to create a powerful focus for a collection of sentences that at first seem to have no relationship at all:

Nobody need speak of a wilderness. Cows have udders and are
    very young.
Not to speak of sweating.
Seats and a guard.
I am ashamed.
I have to take care of myself gently. (106)

"Wilderness," with its disclaimer of "natural" and undomesticated behavior, together with the familiar "cow," help formulate a context that
the overtly physical and emotional words "sweating," "seats," "guard,"
"ashamed," "care," and "gently" reinforce. "Wilderness," like wildness
of all sorts, is simply not to be mentioned. Only the entirely domesti-
cated beasts can survive here—and even they will have udders instead
of breasts and be thought of as entirely innocent. "Sweating" is another
reminder of our uncouth animal nature. The results of such repression,
the confinement of shame, lead invariably to greater arousal.

Whenever Stein is most frank, she seems most aware of her repression. The voices of her own disapproval, her own internal thought
police, are likely to burst into the text at any moment:

Why are holes cool.
All holes are not cool.
Some holes are cool.
Can I mention an exceptional one. (120)

When challenged by this hostile "other," questionable and ambiguous
content represent a policy decision. Each sympathetic reader becomes
a partner in the act of creating meaning as well as concealing it. At the
least, Stein wants to be protected from her own disapproval; at the
most, she would like her legend to replace her self and to be left a
celebrity, converted into a statue like Susan B. Anthony: "We follow
you. Permit me to remain covered. I like that. Many bowed. Some
greeted me" (104).

The act of concealment requires authority: "Authority, in speaking
of an authority we say he says. We like the phrase in a position to
know. We still prefer that the dog looks like a lamb. We change our
minds so often. Do not let us worry about it" (106). Stein seems to be
thinking both of herself, the suspect cur who knows her audience
would prefer a lamb, and her actual pet poodle, Basket, who resembled
a lamb. Writing gives her the authority, with a pun on author, to repel
possible doubts. It puts her "in a position to know," both physical and
literary. If she feels she has overstepped permissible bounds of expressive freedom, she can change her mind or dismiss the entire subject.
But to be understood, she enlists readers' help, asking them to correct
and emend her texts: "Please correct this" (99). Either through correc-
tion or active interpretation, the reader regains the text and learns how
to read it by steering through its contradictions.

These changeable, flexible texts are the charts of her fears and illusions: "Milky way. The translation of this is Saint Augustine. Do not laugh or relate it to the cow. The cow came out. Of course it does it has the habit" (111). The first reference might be sexual, an interpretation further supported by a reference to another "saintly sinner," Saint Augustine, another of Stein's male alter egos. Like Caesar, Byron, and others, Saint Augustine can represent both the unbridled id and the patriarchal power structure of civilization that represses it. Augustine "came burning" but he repented as well. As part of her opposite speech, she presents readers with two alternative ways of reacting to her text. They can either "laugh" and enjoy her words as nonsense, or they can "relate it to the cow" by following the "habit" of her mind. The reader must determine the text, building structures of continuity and possibility.

The reader is invited to shift meanings as the writer circles around related imagery, such as "fire" in the following passage, which connects with some other familiar references: "This sounds like nothing but they are made out of stones. They would do credit to decorations and be witness to a wilderness. Nothing wild rests . . . nothing discharged is murmured . . . beat it beat coals of it. Have a gloomy tooth. Shape it by the fire. The fire has stitches and knows how to sew. By all means be with me" (100). The reader's interpretation is stimulated by partial meanings and a litany of emphatic, rhythmically parallel imperatives that must be extended and refined. The text takes on a definable shape through analysis, replacement, substitution, crossing out, parenthesizing, introducing the forbidden subject in tandem with the author herself: "By all means be with me." If the text proceeds by repetition and contradiction, halting, changing course, qualifying, confusing, denying, it also clarifies and points at a recognizable orientation and line of development. Her disclaimer gives way to opacity (stones do not speak) but also to witnessing the wild, bringing in the idea of "discharging" and "murmuring," creative, self-disclosive terms. If her gloom relates to her fear, the fire is what shapes and informs her text.

The Protected Context of "Stanzas in Meditation"

When it comes to intimate matters, Stein treats her readers in ways strongly reminiscent of her treatment of visitors to her salon. As Catharine R. Stimpson has written: "She appears to have had at least two groups of friends. They might all meet each other, but only some would know about her sexuality, while others would not. Those who were aware did not have to be homosexuals themselves . . . the initiates protected their shared secret through taste, discretion, and silence" (1977, 495).

"Stanzas in Meditation," written concurrently with *The Autobiography of Alice B. Toklas* (Bridgman, 213) from 1932 to 1935, though not published until 1956, is a reprise of the many protective effects Stein practiced both in her life and in her earlier works. In this late, guarded, long poem, she assumes a different tone from that of works written more than a decade earlier. Here, perhaps for the first time, she uniformly maintains her difficult style through a long sequence of stanzas (over 150 pages). While apparently presenting an entirely "proper" and entirely banal series of subjects and events, much of the energy of the text lies beneath the surface of its difficult style in its parodic play with allusions, ambiguity, partial statements, evasions, coding, and other techniques of erotic display. For readers who insist on the meaninglessness of this text, "Stanzas" must become rough going indeed.

Stein's "success" in masking her intentions, even from sophisticated readers, can be seen in recent criticism. Marianne DeKoven admits giving this work "short shrift": "If a work, however long it is or however substantial in the canon it appears, fails to offer anything to a reader, there is no point to pursuing a reluctant analysis" (1983, 107). Richard Kostelanetz, in his Introduction to *The Yale Gertrude Stein* (1980), lists "Stanzas in Meditation" among other difficult texts "entirely eschewing subjects" (xxviii). Yet the passages he cites, including this one from "Before the Flowers of Friendship Faded," are far from being "exemplary" of the "nonsemantic" nature of Stein's difficult writings:

> It is always just as well
> That there is a better bell
> Than that with which a half is a whole
> Than that with which they went away to stay
> Than that with which after any way
> Needed to be gay to-day

The word *gay*, which meant "homosexual" in Stein's era as it does in our own, should provide a sufficient clue. As Paul Ricoeur writes in "Metaphor and the Main Problem of Hermeneutics" (1978), "a clue is a kind of index for a specific construction, both a set of permissions and a set of prohibitions" (142). In this case, it permits the reader to assume that the "better bell" may contain a punning reference to Alice B. Toklas as a "better belle." As Stein's "better" "half," the one who makes her "whole" ("hole"), the one with whom she "went away to stay" in Europe, because she "needed to be gay," Toklas's presence provides the passage with focus and meaning. The missing antecedent of the initial "it" is Stein's relationship to Toklas. The passage is difficult and obscure, but it is not meaningless.

In two key passages from the "Stanzas," the opening of Parts i and ii, Stein concentrates her ideas and displays her contradictory methods. She offers a panoply of possible reader interactions, testing possibilities and orchestrating a range of reactions from her imagined audience. In search of her "rescuing" readers, yet ever wary of rejection and disgrace, Stein remains at once intimate and distanced. In Stanza i, Part i, she begins with typical punning that immediately introduces and qualifies her subject—it is at once an introduction to the "I," a parodic reference to the muse of her inspiration, and a pun with sexual implications. Its style is so characteristic of Stein's difficult texts in its covert display as to be instantly recognizable:

> I caught a bird which made a ball
> And they thought better of it. (3)

When a bird changes to an eroticized "ball," it is disturbing enough to require the entrance of the abstract "they" who seem simultaneously to approve and disapprove.

In Part ii, Stanza i, Stein begins: "Full well I know that she is there":

> Full well I know that she is there
> Much as she will she can be there
> But which I know which I know when
> Which is my way to be there then
> Which she will know as I know here
> That it is now that it is there
>
> . . . .
>
> That it is here that they are there
> They have been here to leave it now
> But how foolish to ask them if they like it (21)

Stein receives support from this relationship, which is simultaneously that between lovers and between the writer and reader. She invokes the forces of repression, mid-sentence and without any preparation— "leave it now"—even as she wills her message to expression. She shows her chosen one, whether lover or reader, her "way," at the same time drawing others away from her content.

The relationship to the mysterious "she" of "Stanzas" soon requires contradictory statements to balance any impropriety. What the couple does and how they feel about it are at issue. The anticipation of repression constitutes an admission of guilt. Her contradictory mode characteristically follows closely upon the act of affirmation. With rhyme and repetition and a warning to the reader, she continues a stubborn, Janus-like response to external judgments:

> And very probably just as well they will have it
> Which they like as they are very likely not to be
> Reminded that it is more than ever necessary
> That they should never be surprised at any one time. (21–22)

What she has received from the relationship must be protected:

> At just what they have been given by taking what they have
> Which they are very careful not to add with (22)

Nonetheless, her situation must be described. Despite all misgivings, the very act of telling remains essential:

> As they can easily indulge in the fragrance
> Not only of which but by which they know
> That they tell them so. (22)

At the nexus of the reader's experience and the writer's narrative, Stein's sympathetic readers will understand and so confirm her identity.

As a whole, "Stanzas in Meditation" presents Stein's characteristic attitudes and content, taking us along several lines of thought simultaneously. There is a hint, even in her most noncommital passages, of an "other" subject, presumably closed, but waiting to be understood. Both reader and writer must manage a difficult narrative—and they can only succeed as cooperative fellow travelers. It is the nature of the reader, after all, that inspires, and is liable for, the true telling.

Because the "I" does speak meaningfully, Stein must be circum-
spect, careful to balance any impropriety. She is the maker of the text
and champion of lesbian identity, but she insistently claims no responsibility for how her writing might be interpreted:

> It is useless to introduce two words between one
> And so they must conceal where they run
> For they can claim nothing
> Nor are they willing to change which they have
> Oh yes I organise this. (29)

She organizes the structure of telling, and she is not "willing to
change." In her last stanzas she tacitly admits the existence of her
dangerous, sexually charged material by "thanking" the reader for not
stopping to interpret it:

> Thank you for hurrying through.
> . . . .
> I call carelessly that the door is open
> Which if they can refuse to open
> No one can rush to close. (151)

A reader may choose not to enter the door, but it will remain open for
the willing readers: "let them be mine" (151). They know "that I
chose" (151) both my narrative and personal style. Even if she misses
connecting with the reader, "the miss is mine" (151), her lifestyle remains intact:

> Because I am coming.
> Certainly I come having come. (151)

For the hostile or indifferent reader, let the poem remain silent: "it is of
no importance," it is not "meant as meaning" (118). "This," she means
us to understand, "is an autobiography in two instances" (76).

6

"In Conversation"
Speaker, Message, and
Receiver

The Speaker: A Split Self

Stein is always aware of the fictitious nature of the category of sexuality to which she has been assigned by birth, but her attempts to unveil the discrepancy are often obscure. The gap between her assigned and her actual sexuality must always be overwhelmed by the force of the real—her woman's body, her knowledge of social prohibitions on lesbianism, her own guilt and prudery about the subject of her discourse, the precariousness of her balance between social tolerance and social rejection. There will always be a difference between what the self knows itself to be and what it can present to the outside world. In Stein's writing, however, her fear of discovery threatens to overwhelm the fragile architecture of her personality: "I cannot say that I ever make a mistake. Conversational" ("I Can Feel the Beauty," PL, 85).

If the speaker cannot unite the different parts of her psyche, she needs at least to "distinguish one listener from the other" ("Nest of Dishes," PL, 103) in order to tailor speech to the level of acceptance. She asks each one, "can you stand description" (104), hoping that the most affirmative and non-judgmental of her opposites in conversation will be "led by their waists their hearts and their ears" (105).

At such moments, Stein's persona posits a utopian setting for conversation in which the members are unrestrained and approving: "He spoke pleasantly indeed humorously, he described not each thing but several things and every one being pleased and excited they expressed their emotions freely. In this way nothing was changed except the illumination" ("Talks to Saints," PL, 112). This kind of scene is part of the idealized persona's vision of the world. This self asserts its unassailability. Such utopian discourse, however, is another fantasy, another fiction. She must know what to watch for and guard against: "I also meant to question every one as to the meaning of startling" ("Yes You Do," PL, 123). She warns even the approving listener and participant in her verbal exchange that "you must consider it as a thing that you have not listened to" (123). And she must apologize to an imaginary Alice B. Toklas: "I had helped to put this silly scruple around her head" ("A New Happiness," PL, 152).

The basic reason Stein's speaker cannot fully place her interlocutor, her "other," is that her identity, as far as her writing is concerned, is split. Her difficult texts develop with an alternating movement of representation and exclusion, showing the doubleness of her motivation even as she represents her thoughts. One part of her utilizes her own unconscious language, while the other censors and distances that language, anticipating the reactions of the audience, of the sometimes loving but always dangerous listeners.

Often, memory and fantasy condense many events into a single scene, collapsing logical sequence into a simultaneous experience, a predominantly defensive organization of ideas: "Indeed everything can be concealed. She can be concealed in having come and having no right she may even be concealed by their satisfaction as well as believing that it is not for pleasure. After which they after all preferred to anything else that they have done" ("Here. Actualities.," PL, 12). Even her satisfaction is vulnerable, for it depends on the disapproving censors believing that her acts do not bring her pleasure—only then may she validate them. Because of the compromised sexuality of the speaker, she elicits "questions" and affirmations—the affirmation of reflection (of at least a part of her) and the affirmation of being seen: "And so question me say that you like and you look like me and that you look at me" ("A Plan for Planting," PL, 14). This is actually a "plan," as she suggests in the title, for "planting" ideas in her listeners' minds—but she must arrange her speech strategies carefully to avert danger: "Astonish you easily astonish you we are back to conversations. Converse about everything. . . . Dear, this is the thing you must remember. If they love each other I suppose he can cross examine. I am free to say that I do not understand it" ("Painted Lace," PL, 7). The speaker both validates and cancels out the message, delivering only that part of meaning that the listener is ready to accept. The sexual self that admits its true subject cannot overtly take its own preoccupation as a norm for all receivers of its message. Yet it is the law of language that it must be spoken to be analyzed—before its significance can be assessed, something must escape, slip out, into consciousness. Suspended in a cacophony of voices, the speaking self must forge its own identity—which Stein's text can never do—before it can properly create a unified language and reside cohesively in speech.

Stein's art of conversation reveals the complexity of a subject caught between its own nature and cultural expectations, between its private desires and the public law. It can never succeed in submitting the forces of the body to the strictures of language. The speaker wants to fix meaning but also to shift it imperceptibly away from its true subject. The "I" can switch identities, even change places with and impersonate the listener. Its messages reveal its instability and the fragmented nature of its awareness. Its shifting center places the speaker in a position of vulnerability: "Heaven sent friend, I forget him . . . now let us attack playful pleasures . . . do we need to be aware of what we have just said . . . I call on you. Does he call on me" ("A Singular Addition," PL, 278). The listener may be angelic, but the speaker is still wary. The listener will help the speaker to "attack" his pleasures, both to criticize them and vigorously enjoy them. Even the act of speaking, of calling upon the other, does not guarantee the recognition of the "I." "He," the speaker, calls on "me," the self, but the self does not acknowledge hearing anything.

Without the proper response, the self cannot affirm the source of its language; the very action of division becomes a statement of the speaker's predicament as well as the definition of female sexuality: "Can a man divide it in two. I do I mean can a man divide it in two as I do. I do divide it into two . . . it happens to him very frequently as he says. Translate this into an exhibition. An exhibition deserves praise and merits it" ("Praises," PL, 123–124). Stein's persona, as above, is ever divided. Prohibitions on verbal display, like the persona's confession, once understood, become an "exhibition." Then, in her typical technique of reversal, one of many ploys in her defensive arsenal, she replaces the sexual exhibition with a literary one, art that deserves praise. This almost magical transformation momentarily shields her assembly of selves, temporarily retrieved and joined for speech, and keeps the text from disintegrating under a weight of contradictory motives and adverse assessments. In the difficult texts, attempts at conversation can either reinforce the distance of the speaker from the listener or establish a covert understanding between the two. Dialogue is forever joined to ambivalence, even when speaker and listener are struggling towards each other: "She was never in pain. Nor in girls. Do sing for girls. Let us all be married together. Can riches mean more then rubbers" ("Nest of Dishes," 99).

> This is not below meaning.
> We will relieve suffering. We can promise anything.
> I can feel that beauty. ("I Can Feel the Beauty," 84–85)

> She was not reminded of a door by a door. Indeed she asked are
>   women engaging. ("Nest of Dishes," 101)

Finding the right voice, the mode that changes monologue into dialogue and speaking into singing, the most sensual form of sound communication, involves readers in a relationship akin to "engagement" and marriage. Reaching such listeners, having them understand, might ironically be more important than actual physical touching, described by the punning "rubbers" ("rub hers"). The "door," though plainly seen, will ostensibly go unrecognized by both writer and reader.

The Message: An Indeterminate Medium

The conversation produced by the divided speaker can never be exactly what she intends—more likely, the message is the material reminder of what the speaker seeks to know: "I speak of all this as if I know it" ("Painted Lace," PL, 6). What is uttered gives rise to even more speculation: "conversation means one talking . . . to another one. One might assume. And say . . . spell treason" (9). The self can be betrayed by its own language. Care is essential. The message is desire, but its real object is missing—the language tells of desire without itself becoming explicitly sexual. Which language should Stein's divided speaker use—one that employs direct references to anatomy and activity, the eroticism of contemporaries like Henry Miller, or a euphemistic usage? Representation invites blame; the message must be quickly deniable. "This prepares their meddling" ("How Are Fears," 140).

Social prohibitions exist to be both rebelled against and obeyed.

The message, implicit or explicit, proves deviation, whether uttered, printed, found, or responded to. Either the acceptance or the obliteration of the message affirms the audience's complicity, whether as lover or censor. The listener agrees either to create meaning or to join in its denial. The result, as Stein knew, was some revolution in the "telling" power of language, one that required new sources, new associations, and new skills from both writer and reader: "Interlude of a dictionary . . . spell wishes at once . . . final . . . felt . . . reality . . . prepared . . . anticipate . . . spell what there is to tell. . . . Spell awake . . . believe . . . cut and follow . . . exact . . . spell trace. . . . They can induce them to do it again" ("Natural Phenomena," PL, 176–77).

This "interlude" of language, spelling the unknown with both letters and incantations, prepares listeners and cues those who are ready to accept the message. It leaves its trace to be discovered—in this case, the "cut," an interesting concept for Stein in terms of both the feminine body and her literary methodology. In its broad reference to the female body, the divided speaker, the powerful internalized censor, the interrupted relationship between writer and reader or speaker and hearer, and the alternating voyages into sense and nonsense, the "cut" is emblematic of Stein's work at its most difficult. Lacan has adopted this same term, using it in ways that strongly recall Stein's own situation: "What Lacan called a 'cut' . . . interrupted statements [that] are not meaningless. . . . It is at such interrupted moments, when meaning stumbles . . . where there is a break in the ego's cohesion, that one may recognize the presence of desire" (Benvenuto and Kennedy, 167). Listeners are "spelled awake" by the new language, transformed by it, induced to participate in it by the very heterogeneity of meaning it represents, by the "erotics of form . . . by the drama of desire" (Brooks, 348). In spite of the couple's shame, the unconscious allows them to form a new language[1]:

> Couples are ridiculous . . . now then.
> Wordless they need not be. ("Practice of Oratory," PL, 138)

Part of Stein's speaker's defense is humor—the humor of the *déclassé* (Jew, woman, lesbian), the perverse bad example. Part of her armory of transmutation is cancellation; part is metaphor; part is non sequitur layering. All of these are present in normal conversation, but in Stein's work the very exclusivity of her idiosyncratic, aberrant usage intensifies

and magnifies her effects, creating the experimental and "cut" surface of
her text: "How can anyone not know this is thunder and more. . . .
Paper and all as useful and find it need it . . . it was . . . an aim . . . a
name. Passing by the standing and in no sense seating place. Otherwise
known as put there. In no sense did the pressing share it. To share it
too. . . . All can admire imitation" ("Geography," PL, 247–50).

With her opening lines, the audience is called to attention, caught
by an odd mixture of expectation and fear. How could anyone not
know the "thunder" of orgasm, the language of "jouissance"?[2] Relief
either comes from the thunder or from the prohibition against it—or
from both at once. Paper will be useful in her campaign of telling, but
there are multiple audiences. The uninitiated will pass by; only the
knowing will share the "seating," what is "put there" and "pressed,"
mirroring the speaker's intention. The reward is a greater awareness of
the malleability of language. Yet the reader comes away with a notion
of a message still unfulfilled, still potential, which challenges not only
the speaker to present it but the receiver to interpret and complete it.

The Object of Communication: "They Seemed to Hear Me"

Language always belongs to another person as well as the self because it is a transmitted, public form. The other, the listener, occupies
the place where meaning falters or even slips: "I said I did. I said it
once when I said it and it made them not only hear me but they seemed
to hear me which they did not . . . anyone can read handwriting and
signs" ("Here. Actualities.," 13). The speaker realizes that there is no
final guarantee or securing of the language of sexuality, as Freud implies when he speaks of the "disjunction between sexual object and
sexual aim" (Mitchell and Rose, 33). And even as the unconscious
severs the self from the physical body, the speaking self cannot be sure
to whom it is speaking.

But as language makes the self, it also forms a relation with the
other. Where these two meet, the self, subject to her own speech, must
acknowledge the other, the object of her discourse. This other, imaged
as male or female, is all the speaker can know of the other: "Why
should they not be anxious. How can they excuse one another"
("Painted Lace," PL, 7).

The speaker's fears are clear, as are her demand for purity, her desire
to be excused, her wish to keep her reputation intact. The self knows

there will never be an unmediated approach to the object of its conversations—desire, gender, situation will determine the nature of its approaches. The object and she are so close—but not facing each other. Distance is a necessary part of their relationship, marking the separation between self and receiver, even though they are superficially the same.

This space between the subject and the object is all potential—there is an active interplay between the speaking self and the other to whom the speech is addressed. This dimension of conversation changes the speech of the self and the other's reaction—they are continually affecting one another. The performance of the speaking self results from a dialectic marked by contradiction:

> This way was the way we did it.
> We resolved to be careful.
> We would not do as she wished.
>
> .   .   .   .
> We are easily careful . . . we said
> what do you want.
>
> .   .   .   .
> We are easily careful.
> They used my name.
>
> .   .   .   .
> Of what and why . . . do we have to be. You know very well why
>   we have to be. Do you mean tomorrow. I mean every day.
> Of what.
> And why.
> I cannot answer questions.
> Can not you. ("Let Us Be Easily Careful," PL, 35–38)

In her opening the speaker portrays her shifting focus. She again wants to exhibit how "it" is done, but in a guarded way. The negation serves as a censor or "third person" in the conversation—the two, the censor and the object, will not do as the speaker wishes. Against a chorus of admonition, the speaker adopts a defensive strategy. Both the censor and the object ask the speaker, What do you want? The speaker, aware of having been found out, balks at necessary defensive tactics. The object and censor are one in assuring her of the wisdom of such ploys. The whole question is again avoided by the speaker's feigned ignorance and by her refusal to be a source of information about the couple, volleying the responsibility back to the listener.

But has the listener learned her lesson well enough to reproduce it in the absence of the speaker? For the motive of the conversations is a call to active participation in the secrets of the speaker's life; the "I" of past action is fused to the "you" of potential future action. The "I" moves from its questionable status as a split self through the unsettling process of communication to the symbolization of the other—from the unconscious to the self in speech to the practice of the other. The imaginary discourse develops from the self to the verbalized representation of its wishes to the listener; eros is the force that makes one of two. Often Stein's speaker fluctuates between this fusion and the rediscovery of her boundaries and limitations. The duplication of female anatomy, the "doubling" that she sees in the beloved, contrasts with her knowledge of her idiosyncratic logic and separate personal identity:

> Do you begin to like whispering.
> You do approve of it.
> No indeed I do not.
> Well then I was mistaken.
> Why do you put it upsidown. I didn't. Didn't you.
> When did you begin this.
> I am very pleased to say so. Intelligence and quick movements and dainty ways. Always. ("I Often Think About Another," PL, 34)

Stein's speaker questions the other about her reaction to the secrets being transmitted. She asks for what the listener can give—approval—and is refused. She withdraws—and then, switching her strategy, accuses the listener of refashioning the material, turning it into the opposite of what the self intended. The listener denies this, suggesting that the reversals are the speaker's fault. This double denial, on both the speaker's and the listener's parts, cancels out prohibited content and allows the conversation to connect the two, even to the point where the speaker embodies an idealized other, imagining her "dainty ways."

Through her discourse the speaking self constructs, condenses, and collapses meaning. The reader, like an analyst of the "borderline" language of patients, is struck by something "alogical, unstitched and chaotic" in Stein's speech patterns—something eroticized, non-communicative, and yet exhibitionistic (Kristeva, 1983, 42).

> An even better way.
> That changes everything.
> When a part of it is in their way and an adaptation.
> . . . .
> At the same time.
> . . . .
> Arrange for it.
> He said no.
> To be as carefully as that . . .
> believing that she might just as well kiss . . .
> . . . .
> Approach as well.
> She as satisfied.
> . . . .
> Remind me.
> . . . .
> On top of this.
> . . . .
> Assist me.
> . . . .
> He imagined he had an object.
> Referring to some one else.
> Distance disturbed, dislike and delight. ("After At Once,"
>   PL, 53–54)

Stein's piece "After At Once" is both polemical and descriptive, attempting a conversation with abrupt shifts and detours. She hints at the lesbian marriage as a "better way," an "adaptation," transforming lifestyle and language. The association is arranged, then refused for purity's sake, causing arguments with the lover-listener and renewed attempts at satisfaction. The speaking self has to be reminded of the relation of text to sexuality, how one is superimposed upon the other. The listener ("referring to someone else") is someone outside the text whom the intimacy of the speaker's assumptions "disturbs," whose dislike is feared, but whose distance must be bridged because it is linked to the speaker's "delight."

Later in the same piece, the speaker analyzes the love relationship she has with the listener in terms of the language she must use to attract her. Here again Stein presents an interesting example of a "cut" text:

An interruption and more than that.
What is it.
Neatly and not yet.
Laughing to-day.
Who knows who knows it.

.   .   .   .

Who does say so.
Candidly. And further and say so. So differently as differently in
    refusal and in refusal and reproach . . .
Did they put it there.
Why as carefully.
Counting.
To count like that. (58)

Speech interrupts and always "means more" than it can say. The receiver of the message asks about this hidden subtext. The speaker draws her on and puts her off, increasing the mystery and gently teasing—"who knows it"? The listener already knows the message, but the speaker will take her further in, against all the negative reactions and off-putting strategies that are the familiar currency of seduction in the conversations. Although the listener is different and acts differently from the speaker, the question of the binding love and sexuality of the pair remains. Of what is this association constituted?

The rhetorical movement of Stein's speaker follows the pattern of "the talking cure" as outlined by Laplanche: excitation, reaction, symbolization, and psychic elaboration (41). The conversations are intrusions into the listener's (and reader's) sphere—involving a moral and aesthetic shock. This provokes a repercussion on the whole organization of the conversation: the speaker retracts, attempts a further intrusion; the message shifts and finally transforms as the receiver of the message adapts to the new transmission. The speaker guides and weaves the contradictory threads to trap the listener and enlist her aid in transforming the communication: "Can you complain to him. What good does it do. . . . She can be taught everything. You mean she is advantageous. We can talk about love. The love of him. The love for him. We can have hysterical feeling" ("I Can Feel the Beauty," PL, 84).

As complaint gives way to love, "a very little meaning makes a change in her" ("Nest of Dishes," 102). This transformational and contrapuntal action embraces both reasoning and evasion, both the sender's optimism and the receptor's reservation about entering into the "hysteria" of love:

I do not argue . . . I say you must behave decently.

. . . .

How can an incantation be finished. By saying that I was not disappointed in meeting her.
Plan a surprise.

. . . .

A great many people are taught pairs. (105)

The above section takes its shape from the aversion of the listener, which causes the speaker to move out of her sexual mode, ending the litany of desire with the meeting, the change, and the pairing of the couple, turning a breakdown in communication into the capitulation of the receiver. The attentive reader can find this identical pattern repeated elsewhere: "I believe urgently in replying . . . that those to be refused would be refused . . . and answered. No one can be more elastic . . . they care . . . to place it all on the tray . . . one with this advantage" ("Yes You Do," 120). Her power to direct the dialogue makes the speaker bold in refusal and in acceptance. The speaker has the advantage because she is the one who pronounces the message: "This is the difference between intention and attention, between neglect and refusal, between words and countenances" ("I Feel a Really Anxious Moment Coming," PL, 238).

Shadings of words reveal different stances of the message, both its inception (its "intention") and the attitude (of "attention") that the listener assumes. The writer-speaker can also tell benign indifference from rejection, or "refusal," on the listener's part. And words can either be affirmed or denied—depending on the speaker's own attitude and how they are accepted (heard)—judging by other's "countenances." "By naming and recreating the universe the artist can escape from the constraints of reality and restore order to a fragmented inner world" (Berman, 199).

"Conversations" order the speaker's universe, designating how messages will be sent and retrieved. This imaginary dialectic focused on the couple's frustrated and satisfied desires plays itself out against a

series of listeners who are themselves divided about erotic content. But
the dialectic of the speaker's demand for love and the testing of desire
against social prohibitions dictates the direction Stein's speaker's conversations will take.

The form of the discourse inevitably determines the nature of the
social tie formed by it. Meaning and information may be subverted in
an attempt to overthrow the linguistic order of the other. The self
constructs her relation to the other through bits and pieces of "cut"
dialogue that are simultaneously traces, pathways into the chaos of the
unconscious, lines of reasoning for the flailing listener to grasp onto.
The alogical rhythm of Stein's speaker's argument reestablishes the
power of the speaking self to produce relations out of stress and disloca-
tion. She escapes from the necessity to resolve meaning but not from
the demand for relationship that is the concomitant of the receiver's
efforts to understand.

The success of the speaker's forays into meaning comes partly from
the balancing of one element in the conversation against another and
the mirroring and repetition that reproduce the self over and over:
"Speak to me . . . read to me . . . the system is made to complete
healing" ("What Does Cook Want to Do," PL, 32). Sometimes this
balancing of elements and mirroring of responses occurs simultaneously, as in

> temper and temperate tempt and refuse.
> Who had made them valid.
> Oh do be generous.
> And delighted. ("Politeness," 144)

Here prohibition and reaction are embedded in the repeated first syllables of the first line—the receiver's temper, the speaker's temperate
approach, her intention, to tempt, and the reaction to temptation, the
possibility of the association being broken off at any point.

> A great many people exchange us.
> . .   .   .
> It is astonishing to me.
> Look at us and we will speak.
> . .   .   .
> Look at us like that.
> She is not angry . . . only anxious. ("Look at Us," PL, 264–65)

Once the speaker and the receiver of the communication have agreed to share meaning, they are creating the message together, participating in the conversation fully, fused ("exchanged"), observed, and ready to meet the world's objections. And once the message's transforming powers have been unleashed, the participants are not surprised at anything: "No one is surprised that that which is sent has been sent and with the choice of sending as if it were to be received. So unequally have astonishment and unalterable recovering astonished the process. I have a weakness for exits . . . and you also . . . as for change of places . . . come again, and as a request. I feel this to be oratory" ("The Practice of Oratory," PL, 125–26). In oratory, the sender always presupposes the receiver. The receiver must recover meaning and identify with the speaker, changing places in the conversation. Either speaker or receiver could leave or return at any moment, Stein asserts, but both are in readiness for the process of exchange from the literal message to the metaphorical one.

The speaker rethinks and reorders her situation through the message, which is then reinterpreted by the receiver, who actively shapes its final form. Stein's speaker transgresses against the laws of morality and linguistic convention, but obeys another set of laws—the listener's and reader's law of limitation of excess. The conversations seem improvised, but they are carefully controlled by the speaker's motives, on the one hand, and the listener's ability to translate, on the other. The conversants are sustained on either side by social restrainst and self-censorship:

> What a room.
> What a place.
> What a pressure. ("A New Happiness," PL, 159)

The pressure to conform works continually on the efforts at rebellion that fuel the conversations:

> To agree about it is one way to say that they like it to be as it is.
> . . . .
> Did he and all of them resemble her.
> Down it.
> Phenomena of Nature, and down it.
> . . . .
> We went down it.
> . . . .
> Aroused as equal to anything. ("Natural Phenomena," PL, 178–82)

As with the mythical power of love, once the conversation is begun, it is capable of great feats of creativity. It is drawn from "Nature," the Freudian id, and culture, the socialized self. Its pleasure can exist on the linguistic as well as the physical level. The mental play with language echoes the subversion of the communication process (the downing of the other's defenses, the going down to libido, even as the couple agree to suppress, or "down," the shared message). The "we" have mutually entered into the wordlessness of passion and returned to chart the path of excess.

Covert Alliances

The question of covert alliances, both sexual and literary, occupies a central position in Stein's "difficult texts." In *Painted Lace*, as elsewhere, the model of the homosexual couple serves as both parody and paradigm for the successful relationship between the writer and the reader. Both require sympathy, discretion, and support from each partner. In both, the problem of relationships, of sexual freedom, is also the problem of freedom of expression.

Assuming the primacy of sexuality, Stein proceeds according to a particular method. She depends on the reader's capacity to establish the conceptual and expressive meanings of nonconventional texts. But like the association and identity of the homosexual couple in Stein's larger society, the association of meaning and text is necessarily covert and disguised. The complexity of the tie Stein felt with Alice B. Toklas and the resistance to social and sexual norms it represented reinforce her evasive narrative strategies.

One convincing evidence of the intentionality of Stein's difficult style is the satiric wit that punctuates the surface jangle of her linguistic maneuverings and veerings off from the subject: "We satisfy the longing for a solitude à deux" ("A Sonatina Followed by Another" BTV, 29); "A special name for careless is caress" (14).

Neither beloved nor reader is long allowed by Stein to forget the need to preserve a measure of prudent reticence and restraint, the recognition that powerful taboos limit but do not preclude the public expression of Stein's deepest feelings. Stein is referring to the couple perhaps, when she explains: "It should be a lesson to them . . . not to be so thin not to be so stout not to be so ready to shout not to be so ready to go about" ("To Do" AB, 69). Though Stein here seems to mock the very idea of the couple (Toklas thin, Stein stout), her defen-

siveness is fused with evident deep affection. Stein's feelings of isola-
tion and hesitancy about speaking of the relationship are understand-
able and even poignant. These comments reflect Stein's internalization
of society's disapproval of homosexuality, its absolute prohibition of
descriptions of physical acts, and its devaluation of women.

Like the neurotic described by Ellie Ragland-Sullivan, who asks
himself his "secret and stifled question—'Am I man or woman?' "
(285)—Stein's speaker must equivocate about the most basic compo-
nent of her sexual identity: "The only letter that can make you know
that you are you is burned away" ("To Do" AB, 78). Under these
conditions the covert alliance of the homosexual couple can serve as a
paradigm for the reader/writer relationship; through her intersubjec-
tive dialogue, Stein's speaking self hopes to identify an affirming presence among the host of her potential critics.

The possible sharing of sensibility between sympathetic reader and
secretive writer in "All Sunday" helps define the terms of Stein's
stylistic experimentation. The self must be mixed with and marked by
the other, mirrored, merged, and even exchanged. "Alone together"
(AB, 89), mirroring is often presented in a ritualistic fashion: "by
exchanging courtesies, by bowing by being impressive, by impressing"
(94); "By imitating a voice I hear it" (94); "Do be copied by me. / I was
so astonished . . . we make an excuse of the way" (96). The particular
quality of this arrangement is its passive appearance of ritualized interaction without the loss of specific erotic content.

The same characteristic amalgam of intention and discretion is evident in each of the following passages, where the acceptance of the
couple, and hence the self, is embedded in negation, first literary, and
then social: "I could say another word. Who wishes it. Not that . . . the
young man told us that he understood from the words that there . . .
were frightful messages" (91); "They wanted to be polite so they did
not ask if she was my sister. One never says that" (110). The unsympathetic reader can keep the couple from being discovered through his or
her own kind of negation, refusing to ask the obvious questions, just as
the writer need not embarrass her "others" by speaking too openly of
her desire. The presence of desire, however, is always assumed, never
debatable, even if its expression must be guarded.

If the couple and their actions arouse guilt, then so does the creative
process itself (Rank, 43). Stein must "practice caution" ("A Sonatina
Followed by Another" BTV, 30), but, as Kristeva has pointed out,
language "brings desire into being by its very structure" (1980, 28).

Under the couple's placid air of satisfaction passion waits, an abyss of emotion that never loses its connection with the ones who created it. And the enjoyment of the couple is never driven out of the speaker's discourse.

Denial, as Freud has asserted, is a "form of avowal" (Muller and Richardson, 269). Through interpretation we come to understand that "I do not like to say it" ("All Sunday," 101); "I am so disturbed" (114). Yet even when she is saying "I consider it a mistake" (114–15), the excluded and negated material in the speaker's repertoire returns, refashioned, again and again: "We were not fooled by the skin. Oh no" (115); "Blandishments are long" ("A Sonatina Followed by Another," 4).

Stein's speakers almost always provide a larger framework for their preoccupations. The reader is left with an undeniable sense of the sexual and feminine that overrides any immediate uncertainty, as in these two passages from "Miguel": "A best chance is with the tool and long bedrooms are divided really divided uttering the tune. . . . Then the purse then the tiled rubber roof is collision and really what is fur, fur is summer" (BTV, 38). Here folkloric, architectural, automotive, animal, and natural images remind the reader of the bawdy anatomical context Stein's speaker is capable of expressing. The "tool," mentioned frequently in both "All Sunday" and "In Pebico," meets "long bedrooms," the couple's sexual anatomy—replete with the music of orgasm. Images of "purse" and "rubber" do not appear nonsensical when combined with the collision of two bodies, the "fur" covering, and the heat of passion. In the same section Stein goes on to recapitulate the terms of her confession. The specific words are different, but the structure of meaning is similar; the reader finds still more synonyms for the partner, the instrument, and the enjoyment: "A little date pretty with a log . . . with a cow . . . that repeats . . . the call of the untamed harbor and legs and everything" (38). The sexual organ, although secret, is enjoyed and described admiringly, even seductively, as "most moist, a real wheel" ("In" BTV, 46). Stein's persona jokes about the fat lover's physique in "Press Tons. Press but tons" (50). She can reverse this antic mode and stress the liberating function of sexuality, as in "It is civil . . . remarkable and open . . . the tread all bed" (51).

The reader, like the lover, can find many synonymous expressions for the images of desire, such as a "pocket" ("Lifting Belly" BTV, 70); "case" (the punning "wear in a case," "In," 50); "precious center lay lips" ("Oval," itself an "organ image," BTV, 121); and "package . . . suddenness" (the act and the image, intertwined, 129). Action and image combine once more in the command "end into a seam" (130) and the self-congratulatory "neat shelter chose" (133). The persona even attempts explanations in "reason for a crate" (140) and excuses in "loud extra. Allowed extra" (133). These images are not polemical, but they do indicate approval and arousal. Predictably, the site of innermost desire is hidden, wrapped, sealed away, sewn, sheltered. But it would be immodestly naive to deny the representational qualities of such texts. Even seemingly neutral words and phrases can be read as pointed commentary.

Desire, act, and art are the inextricable circumstances of Stein's covert alliance. Though the speaker often begins a sequence discussing the creative act by gesturing toward the lover, demanding something, it is the reader she is also gesturing toward. Writing anticipates "the next occasion for reaching" ("Birth and Marriage" AB, 183), after which the persona will "make a diary of having asked her" ("A Diary" AB, 213), hoping that "she wants to read it" ("A History or Messages from History," AB, 222).

Stein's personae, asking, writing, even "singing," remain attentive to their lovers' reactions. The characteristic movement from self to other and back to self again defines the basic narrative strategy of her "difficult" texts. By accepting her desire in its artistic form, the reader validates Stein's identity and excuses her for any violations: "I address my caress . . . to the one . . . who blesses me" ("A Sonatina Followed by Another" BTV, 6). The desiring language is so inextricably intertwined with the excusing language that the one transforms and makes the other possible.

Stein's instinct is that words and images can make the transition from their origin in desire to other meanings and values and back again. Meanwhile, the practical terms of the argument evade both expectations and prohibitions:

> Useful enough for that much. Do you remember that a pump can pump other things than water. For this search the land. Yes tenderness grows and it grows where it grows. And do you like it. Yes you do. And does it fill a cow full of filling. Yes. And where does it come out of. It comes out of the way of the Caesars . . . rich in thought and in deed. Indeed.
> Coming in at the door.
> Shut the door.
> Yes. (26)

In this passage, metaphors of instruments, food, treasure, and architecture crowd the speaker's confession about desire and act, but she does not hesitate to close off discussion at the moment of knowledge (the "coming"), with the respondent's ambiguous consent.

Desire, separate from function and even participants, is firmly entrenched in the speaker's metaphoric repertoire: "This is talk. Plain grease in covers" ("Bee Time Vine," 36). Paradoxically, for Stein's speaker's desire to succeed, it must "cover" itself: "No taste in two. / No twine in two and a best set. / Coal hole" (35). Here the couple have no obvious affect or connection, but the "set" they represent has a source of passion that, if hidden, still harbors a fierce energy conveyed by "moist neglected pens full of understanding" (35).

In "Lifting Belly," the very title revels in acts: "I know the title . . . we have made no mistake" (83). Eating dominates the persona once more, this time in a specifically sexual context; "eat the little girl I say" (83). She tells the audience they "are excited" (82) to be a "witness" to her "wolfish" nature (99). She asks for permission to "prepare" the lover (99).

In "Lifting Belly," the power of the persona in the act is fraught with responsibilities. The writing is a "reminder of present duties" (100), and the act of love an "emergency" requiring powers normally kept "in reserve" (103). But the persona must never seem oppressed—"can you sing at your work" (115). She also speaks of her identity as a "melody member" of the couple ("Oval" BTV, 119).

The quiet domestic metaphors like "sewing," often used by Stein to connote touching, become more reckless in "Oval." The persona performs a "churning . . . loud hemstich" with "spit" and a "naughty spoon" (119). "Let the place call," she declares. With protestations of "offal" and "murder," the persona nonetheless becomes a "tender toe binder," a "mover around ridiculous" (119). By the writing, a "ray" on acts, the reader can voyeuristically "peep" at the scene, a "ram" (119–20). The gaze must be averted when, with a possible pun on "Lev-ite," the persona orders: "Disappear . . . leave eye. / Pollute" (120).

Why the curious, violent imagery that dominates "Oval"? There, as elsewhere, the play of Stein's imaginative demands produces a rhythm of growing expectation, a vocabulary of imperatives for the other to follow:

In a lean.
Not noisy.
Feel rail.
Rest.
Roll.
Right.

To shown.

· · · · · ·

Arouses.

· · · · · ·

Erect.

· · · · · ·

It was a rendering.

· · · · · ·

Knee sew.
An in mine.
Commending. (135)

In her first identity she gives instructions to her beloved. Speaking about herself, she comments on her ability (to "arouse"), which reminds her of male sexual imagery ("erect"). The humorous "knee sew" reminds the reader of the polymorphous sexuality of the female body, capable of arousal at all points. The function of the writing is to show, producing acceptance and praise.

Of all the words that have a sexual connotation, perhaps the word "in," often part of a fragmented phrase, as above, gathers most significance through repeated mention. It can be a description of place (an inn?) or a litany of shame and desire, both in the same piece: "shame on in" (145). Elsewhere the object of "in" is recessed, disguised as "crater," "spore," "core," or "space" ("Meal One" BTV, 148), "hoop" or "barrel" ("Why Can" BTV, 192). The acts that join lover to place are distanced, separate, aggressive and polite by turns: "break . . . usher . . . elevate . . . pierce" ("Meal One," 148).

Only Stein's variable persona could speak of "that work" ("Why Can," 191) even while she queries the reader uneasily, "can you say lapse" (192). She has no means of directly discussing her subject, even her gender—"Can you see her dressed or him" (190). Although the couple "cannot conceal" ("Can You" BTV, 205), they do have the comfort of inhabiting a text where "lust is not a name" (204). If the couple are "careful together" ("Why Win Things" BTV, 205), they can "play . . . men" ("In Their Play" BTV, 206).

The codes of desire, repeated throughout these texts, assemble in a litany that endures comprehensibly, within and despite all surface difficulties, dislocations, "mistakes," and confusions. The domain of this discourse is the intimacy of the couple. If the reader can accept Stein's celebration of her passions, the writer will be eloquent.

Notes

■

Chapter 1

1. *The Mother of Us All* was published in *Last Operas and Plays* (1949); although the date given for completion in Bridgman is 1946 (341), as early as 1944 it is being discussed as in process (Simon 232). Its special subject matter implies a kind of "summing up" of experience.

2. About her time in medical school, Stein reports with distaste in *The Autobiography of Alice B. Toklas* that "she had to take her turn in the delivering of babies" (101). Linda Simon also discusses Stein's "aversion to childbirth" (170).

3. Although the title of the piece in the Yale Series is *Two: Gertrude Stein and Her Brother*, Stein's original title was simply *Two*.

4. Some commentators complain about what Pierre Roche called "those damned repetitions" in John Malcolm Brinnin, *The Third Rose*, 150, but Frederick Hoffman calls repetition "her essential stretegy" in *Gertrude Stein* (Minneapolis: University of Minnesota Press, 1961), 20; Brinnin thought it inevitably resulted in "a dead end" (142). Norman Weinstein, in *Gertrude Stein and the Literature of Modern Consciousness*, 94, suggests that Stein uses her syntax as a mantra or hypnotic religious chant; Bruce Kawin, in *Telling It Again and Again*, feels repetition helps Stein to reach her "most immediate and inaccessible . . . memory . . . to relieve unmastered material" (17). Stein herself in her *Lectures in America* (1935; Boston: Beacon Press, 1957) rejected the term *repetition*, preferring to use *insistence:* "Is there repetition or is there insistence. I am inclined to think there is no such thing as repetition. . . . There can be no repetition because the essence of that expression is insistence, and if you insist you must each time use emphasis and if you use emphasis it is not possible . . . [to] use exactly the same emphasis" (166–67).

5. Otto Fenichel, speaking of a patient, comments on fantasies of this type, in which a woman imagines herself part of a man (and psychoanalytically, that part becomes the penis): "Thus she is inseparably united with him, only a part of him but the most important part," "The Symbolic Equation: Girl = Phallus," *The Collected Papers of Otto Fenichel: Second Series* (New York: Norton, 1954), 6. On the idea of the "resemblance," Fenichel introduces the

concept of the "phallic girl," who identifies with the male not only by saying "I also want to have a penis," but by the formulation "I have seized the penis and eaten it and have now myself become a penis" (4–5). Note a longer quote from the same section of *Two:* "She was the particle and the resemblance and she had the edible piece when she did not eat more than she received" (125).

6. In a letter to A.C. Barnes, Leo declares that "she [Gertrude] is basically stupid and I'm basically intelligent" (*Journey Into Self*, 149).

7. He indicates that finality in his comment on his move in a 1913 letter to Mabel Weeks: "This domestic discord has had its importance in urging what Alice's coming has facilitated, my freeing myself from what was in any serious way a check on my independence . . . in many ways freedom has come to me" (*Journey Into Self*, 53).

8. Whether Leo was actually happier than Gertrude or happier without her for the rest of his life after the break in 1913 is open to question, but there are indications in his autobiography *Journey Into Self* and in the various biographies of Gertrude Stein that he was bitter about her greater success, which he felt was undeserved. Writing to Mabel Weeks, he called Gertrude's writing "the worst Godalmighty rubbish that is to be found" (53).

9. The manuscript has been collated and arranged by letters and numbers, which I have reproduced. I am not certain that it is completely chronological—it seems to have been thematically organized to some extent.

10. Sarah Stein was a serious artist who, at the time of Gertrude's arrival, was already taking classes under Matisse. With her husband, she hosted a salon that was a meeting place for important modern artists who became friends of Gertrude as well. Ulla Dydo asserts that Sarah Stein represents the female half of *Two* in "Must Horses Drink. or, 'Any Language Is Funny If You Don't Understand It,' " 276.

11. Catharine Stimpson writes in depth about this symbiosis in "Gertrice/Altrude: Stein, Toklas, and the Paradox of the Happy Marriage."

12. Several key ideas in this section are drawn from Janine Chasseguet-Smirgel's *Creativity and Perversion*, in which she compares the function of aestheticized objects and fetishes. Here I am paraphrasing from page vii, where she explicates her general theory.

13. Chasseguet-Smirgel discusses the patient's magical identification with the "parental universe" (93).

14. Both Alice B. Toklas and Gertrude Stein knew Annette Rosenshine well; Stein took her up as a protégé, "an interesting subject for observation" (Simon, 58). Stein had read Alice's letters to Annette a year before she met Alice in 1907. Annette was dropped when Stein and Toklas established their relationship, and she returned to San Francisco in 1908.

15. Bridgman (151) explores the image of "cow" in "Bee Time Vine" and "Painted Lace." This is also detailed in Simon's Appendix, "An Annotated Gertrude Stein," in the section "A Word About Caesars and Cows."

Chapter 2

1. Walter Sorell, *Three Women* (Indianapolis: Bobbs-Merrill, 1975), 107–8, writes of Stein as "making a most desperate attempt not to let us know the real aspects of reality" and of her not having "admitted to herself . . . the degree of intensity with which she tried to shield herself."

2. "Caesar" was one of Stein's pet names for male power; Stimpson (1985) observes that "as Roman, Stein could also be 'mannish' without any direct declaration of lesbianism" (71). Also see Bridgman: "[The Caesars] appear repeatedly as custodians and masters of ceremonies for the cow" (152); "they make the most sense as parts of the body, physical acts, and character traits" (152).

3. "The dialogue was often an inner one carried on between Gertrude Stein and

herself. The drama was minimal . . . the norm is regularly re-established . . . it is impossible to determine whether the dialogue is between Gertrude Stein and another, or between Gertrude Stein and herself. Long portions seem to be verbalized inner monologues, broken by external exchanges" (Bridgman, 141–42).

4. Donald Sutherland, in *Gertrude Stein: A Biography of Her Work*, observes: "One should be as intellectually direct and ready as a child or a saint, with a flair for the impossible, for coincidences and collisions, for puns, paradoxes, slapstick, and the outrageous . . . a great deal of the work of Gertrude Stein can quite fairly be taken as a sort of Wonderland or Luna Park for anybody who is not too busy" (83–84).

5. "The 'cow' is associated with food, with wetness, and with an emergence, which on one occasion is not unlike birth" (Bridgman, 151). See also Linda Simon, "Cows seem to be synonymous with orgasms" (317). In her Appendix Simon encodes several phrases from "Lifting Belly" and "A Sonatina Followed by Another."

Chapter 3

1. Martin Harrow and Mel Prosen, "Intermingling and Disordered Logic as Influences on Schizophrenic 'Thought Disorders,' " *Archives of General Psychiatry* 35 (1978): 1213. "Disordered thinking," they write, "is believed by most clinicians and theorists to be the central or fundamental feature of schizophrenia." Psychiatrists often use the phrases "anomalous word strings" and "random thought trains" to characterize deviance in schizophrenic utterance. Stein was entirely conscious of the experimental unorthodoxy of her style, including the deliberate deformations of, and departures from, conventional language. The psychoanalytic literature cited here and following is meant only to establish a useful vocabulary for describing Stein's difficult texts; it is not meant to suggest that Stein herself was schizophrenic.

2. Bertram D. Cohen, Gilead Nachmani, and Seymour Rosenberg, in "Referent Communication Disturbances in Acute Schizophrenia," *Journal of Abnormal Psychology* 83 (1974): 2, provide two models for communication in which "the speaker implicitly takes the role of listener in order to 'test' the adequacy of a sampled response before emitting (or rejecting) it." A self-editing function of this type is reminiscent of Sullivan's (1946) conception of the "fantastic auditor" and Mead's (1934) conception of the "generalized other." "The function of this type of mechanism is to edit out utterances the speaker judges to be inappropriate . . . before they intrude into overt speech." Later they demonstrate how a schizophrenic's comparison and sampling procedure may deviate from that of a normal speaker (3): "[The schizophrenic] samples from an idiosyncratic repertoire and bases his comparison stage judgments on correspondingly deviant associative strengths . . . if [he] tests his utterances . . . against idiosyncratic norms . . . his response will fail to communicate accurately" (3).

3. Elaine Chaika, in "A Linguist Looks at 'Schizophrenic Language,' " *Brain and Language* 1 (July 1974): 272, discusses "intrusive word associations" as one of the characteristic features of schizophrenic thought, along with lack of coherence, redundancy, frequent punning, and rhyming. The same author also considers punning as a kind of intrusion, "the deliberate assigning of the wrong semantic features for the context to a particular item in the lexicon" (264–65). This is contrary to the views of Harrow and Prosen, who see schizophrenic intrusions as the " 'intermingling' of material into . . . verbalizations at a point . . . when it was inappropriate" (1217).

4. Brendan Maher, in "The Language of Schizophrenia: A Review and Interpretation," *British Journal of Psychiatry* 120 (1972): 8, writes that "frequent repetitions at smaller intervals is characteristic of schizophrenic subjects . . . repetition is evidence of excessive rigidity and need for security and should be interpreted as an anxiety-reducing symptom."

5. Marianne DeKoven, in "Gertrude Stein and Modern Painting: Beyond Literary

Cubism," writes that Gertrude Stein and modern painting "both shatter or fragment perception and the sentence (canvas), and both render multiple perspectives" (82).

6. Chaika speaks of Vetter's theory of "word salads" as "made out of recognizable words that seem unrelated to each other" ("Schizophrenic Language," 266). In a later article, Chaika gives Lorenz's example of a "word salad" as "the honest bring back to life doctors agents much take John Black out through making up design meaning straight neutral underworld and shadow tunnel" ("Schizophrenic Speech, Slips of the Tongue, and Jargonaphasia," *Brain and Language* 4 [1977]: 466).

7. Chaika argues that "knowing what must be (and cannot be) overtly stated is an integral part of being able to use the rules of discourse" ("Schizophrenic Language," 273–74).

8. Bruno Callieri and Luigi Frighi, in "Ways of Understanding the Verbal Communication of Schizophrenia," *Human Context* 13 (July 1971): 293–306, discuss redundancy, abbreviation, circumlocutions, and circuit words as modalities of avoidance in schizophrenic speech, as well as coding, role and key perturbation, circular logic, variable and vague relationships between sign and referent, breakdown in communication, hallucinations, obsessions, glossomania, declamatory litanies, metalanguage, and other categories of schizophrenic language.

9. A lack of certainty about the speaker's own identity is reflected in possible multiple personalities. See Chaika's analysis of a schizophrenic speaker from the Kisker tapes ("Schizophrenic Language").

10. A lack of certainty on the part of the speaker about the tone and mood to employ, an example of what Chaika has called "an inability to assess the social situation properly" (274).

Chapter 4

1. The only organizational requirement of *Useful Knowledge* was that the publisher should "make it all the short things she had written about America" ("The Autobiography of Alice B. Toklas," in *Selected Writings of Gertrude Stein*, 227). The pieces in *Useful Knowledge* range from her Majorcan experiences to her postwar preparation for the autobiographies she would publish during the next decade.

2. William Gass, in *World Within the Word*, observes, "The manifest texts contain a coded commentary on the covert texts" (92).

3. "The later stage in the development of the neurotic's estrangement from his parents. . . . might be described as 'the neurotic's family romance,' " Sigmund Freud, *Collected Papers* 5, ed. James Strachey (New York: Basic Books, 1959), 75.

Chapter 6

1. In *Four Fundamental Concepts of Psychoanalysis*, Lacan notes the tendency of the unconscious to allow language to formulate desire even as it swallows it up: "Everything that for a moment appears in its slit (the slit of the unconscious) seems to be destined by a sort of pre-emption to close up again upon itself . . . to vanish, to disappear" (43); "the unconscious is always manifested as that which vacillates in a split in the subject, from which emerges a discovery that Freud compares with desire" (28).

2. Lacan's use of the word *jouissance* for sexual enjoyment carries with it spiritual connotations; see Julia Kristeva, *Desire in Language* (New York: Columbia University Press, 1980), 16.

Works Cited

Barthes, Roland. *The Pleasure of the Text*. Trans. Richard Miller. New York: Hill and Wang, 1975.

Benstock, Shari. "Beyond the Reaches of Feminist Criticism: A Letter from Paris." *Feminist Issues in Literary Scholarship*. Ed. Shari Benstock. Bloomington: Indiana University Press, 1987.

———. *Women of the Left Bank: Paris, 1900–1940*. Austin: University of Texas Press, 1986.

Benvenuto, Bice, and Roger Kennedy. *The Works of Jacques Lacan: An Introduction*. London: Free Association Press, 1986.

Berman, Jeffrey. *The Talking Cure: Literary Representations of Psychoanalysis*. New York: New York University Press, 1985.

Bridgman, Richard. *Gertrude Stein in Pieces*. New York: Oxford University Press, 1970.

Brinnin, John Malcolm. *The Third Rose: Gertrude Stein and Her World*. Boston: Little, Brown, 1959.

Brooks, Peter. "The Idea of a Psychoanalytic Literary Criticism." *Critical Inquiry* 13 (Winter 1987): 334–70.

Chasseguet-Smirgel, Janine. *Creativity and Perversion*. New York: Norton, 1984.

Chessman, Harriet Scott. *The Public is Invited to Dance: Representation, the Body, and Dialogue in Gertrude Stein*. Stanford: Stanford University Press, 1989.

Clement, Catherine. *The Lives and Legends of Jacques Lacan*. New York: Columbia University Press, 1983.

Cook, Blanche Wiesen. "Women Alone Stir My Imagination: Lesbianism and the Cultural Tradition." *Signs: Journal of Women in Culture and Society* 4 (1979): 718–39.

DeKoven, Marianne. *A Different Language: Gertrude Stein's Experimental Writing*. Madison: University of Wisconsin Press, 1983.

———. "Gertrude Stein and Modern Painting: Beyond Literary Cubism." *Contemporary Literature* 22, 1 (Winter 1981): 81–93.

Dydo, Ulla E. "Must Horses Drink. or, 'Any Language Is Funny If You Don't Understand It.' " *Tulsa Studies in Women's Literature* 4:2 (1985): 272–80.

Gass, William H. *The World Within the Word.* Boston: Nonpareil Books, 1979.

Hoffman, Michael J. *Gertrude Stein.* Boston: Twayne Publishers, 1976.

———, ed. *Critical Essays on Gertrude Stein.* Boston: G. K. Hall, 1986.

Kawin, Bruce. *Telling It Again and Again.* Ithaca: Cornell University Press, 1972.

Kristeva, Julia. *Desire In Language: A Semiotic Approach to Literature and Art.* Ed. Leon S. Roudiez. Trans. Thomas Gora, Alice Jardine, and Leon S. Roudiez. New York: Columbia University Press, 1980.

———. "Within the Microcosm of the 'Talking Cure.' " *Interpreting Lacan.* Ed. Joseph H. Smith and William Kerrigan. Trans. Thomas Gora and Margaret Waller. New Haven: Yale University Press, 1983, 33–47. Vol. 6 of *Psychiatry and the Humanities.* Ed. Joseph Smith, vols. 1–12, 1976–90.

Lacan, Jacques. *Four Fundamental Concepts of Psychoanalysis.* Trans. A. Sheridan. New York: Norton, 1977.

———. *Speech and Language in Psychoanalysis.* Baltimore: Johns Hopkins University Press, 1968.

Laplanche, Jean. *Life and Death in Psychoanalysis.* Baltimore: John Hopkins University Press, 1976.

Laplanche, Jean, and J. B. Pontalis. *The Language of Psychoanalysis.* Trans. Donald Nicholson. New York: W. W. Norton, 1974.

MacCannell, Juliet Flower. *Figuring Lacan: Criticism and the Cultural Unconscious.* Lincoln: University of Nebraska Press, 1986.

Mellow, James. *Charmed Circle: Gertrude Stein and Company.* New York: Holt, Rinehart and Winston, 1974.

Mitchell, Juliet, and Jacqueline Rose, eds. *Feminine Sexuality: Jacques Lacan and the Ecole Freudienne.* Trans. Jacqueline Rose. New York: W. W. Norton, 1982.

Muller, John P., and William J. Richardson. *Lacan and Literature: A Reader's Guide to Ecrits.* New York: International Universities Press, 1982.

Perloff, Marjorie. "Poetry as Word-System: The Art of Gertrude Stein." *American Poetry Review* 8:5 (Sept./Oct. 1979), 33–43.

Porter, Katherine Anne. "Gertrude Stein: A Self-Portrait." *Harpers* 195 (Dec. 1947): 519–27.

Ragland-Sullivan, Ellie. *Lacan and the Philosophy of Psychoanalysis.* Urbana: University of Illinois Press, 1986.

Rank, Otto. "Life and Creation." *Literature and Psychoanalysis.* Ed. Edith Kurzweil and William Phillips. New York: Columbia University Press, 1983.

Ricoeur, Paul. *The Philosophy of Paul Ricoeur.* Ed. Charles E. Regan and David Stewart. Boston: Beacon Press, 1978.

Ruddick, Lisa. "A Rosy Charm: Gertrude Stein and the Repressed Feminine." Hoffman, *Critical Essays,* 225–40.

Schmitz, Neil. *Of Huck and Alice: Humorous Writing in American Literature.* Minneapolis: University of Minnesota Press, 1983.

Secor, Cynthia. "Gertrude Stein: The Complex Force of Her Femininity." *Woman, the Arts, and the 1920s in Paris and New York.* Ed. Kenneth W. Wheeler and Virginia Lee Lussier. New Brunswick: Rutgers University Press, 1982, 27–35.

———. "Ida, A Great American Novel." *Twentieth Century Literature* 24, no. 1 (1978): 96–107.

———. "The Question of Gertrude Stein." *American Novelists Revisited: Essays in Feminist Criticism.* Ed. Fritz Fleischmann. Boston: G.K. Hall, 1982.

Simon, Linda. *The Biography of Alice B. Toklas.* New York: Doubleday, 1977.

Stein, Gertrude. *Everybody's Autobiography.* New York: Random House, 1937.

———. *Geography and Plays.* 1922. New York: Something Else Press, 1968.

———. *How To Write.* 1931. New York: Dover, 1975.

———. *Ida.* 1941. New York: Cooper Square Press, 1971.

————. *Last Operas and Plays*. Ed. Carl Van Vechten. New York: Rinehart, 1949.

————. *Narration: 4 Lectures*. Chicago: University of Chicago Press, 1935.

————. *Operas and Plays*. Paris: Plain Editions, 1932.

————. *Selected Writings of Gertrude Stein*. Ed. Carl Van Vechten. New York: Random House, 1945.

————. *Useful Knowledge*. 1929. New York: American Alpine Club, 1972.

————. *Wars I Have Seen*. New York: Random House, 1945.

————. *Yale Gertrude Stein*. Ed. Richard Kostelanetz. New Haven: Yale University Press, 1980.

————. *Yale Series of the Unpublished Writings of Gertrude Stein*. Ed. Carl Van Vechten. 7 vols. New Haven: Yale University Press, 1951–58.

Stein, Leo. *Journey Into the Self*. Ed. Edmund Fuller. New York: Crown Publishers, 1950.

Stimpson, Catharine R. "Gertrice/Altrude: Stein, Toklas, and the Paradox of the Happy Marriage." *Mothering the Mind*. Ed. Ruth Perry and Martine Watson Brownley. New York: Holmes and Meier, 1984.

————. "Gertrude Stein and the Transposition of Gender." *The Poetics of Gender*. Ed. Nancy K. Miller. New York: Columbia University Press, 1986.

————. "The Mind, the Body, and Gertrude Stein," *Critical Inquiry* 3:3 (Spring 1977): 489–506.

————. "The Somagrams of Gertrude Stein." *Poetics Today* 6, 1–2 (1985): 67–80.

Sutherland, Donald. *Gertrude Stein: A Biography of Her Work*. New Haven: Yale University Press, 1951.

Weinstein, Norman. *Gertrude Stein and the Literature of Modern Consciousness*. New York: Ungar, 1970.

Wilson, Edmund. *Axel's Castle*. New York: Scribner's, 1931.

————. *The Shores of Light: A Literary Chronicle of the Twenties and Thirties*. New York: Farrar, Straus, and Cudahy, 1952.

Index